This book will challenge ~~...~~
the image of Christ in th~~... ... ... ...~~

STAN TOLER
Best-selling author, *Stan Toler's Practical Guide for
    Pastoral Ministry* and *The Buzzards Are Circling, but
    God's Not Finished with Me Yet*
Pastor, Trinity Church of the Nazarene in Oklahoma
    City, Oklahoma


We all have a place in the Body of Christ, and John
Jackson's book *Finding Your Place in God's Plan* will
help you find it. It is clear and easy to understand and
a fantastic tool for an individual or for churches.

BOB ROBERTS JR
Senior Pastor, NorthWood Church
Author, *Real-Time Connections, Transformation*, and
    *Glocalization*

# Finding Your Place in God's Plan

# FINDING YOUR PLACE
## IN
# GOD'S PLAN

JOHN JACKSON

Transforming lives through God's Word

## Transforming lives through God's Word

Biblica provides God's Word to people through translation, publishing, and Bible engagement in Africa, Asia Pacific, Europe, Latin America, Middle East, and North America. Through its worldwide reach, Biblica engages people with God's Word so that their lives are transformed through a relationship with Jesus Christ.

Biblica Publishing
We welcome your questions and comments.

1820 Jet Stream Drive, Colorado Springs, CO 80921 USA
www.Biblica.com

Finding Your Place in God's Plan
ISBN-13: 978-1-60657-083-8

A catalog record for this book is available through the Library of Congress.

Printed in the United States of America

# ACKNOWLEDGMENTS

The good people of LifePoint Church (www.lifepointnv.com) were the original laboratory for testing these materials. I am deeply grateful for the kindness and grace of the staff, board, and ministry leaders of my home church. I want to specifically thank Steve and Kirsten Wilson for working with me on this book while they were on the staff. Their contribution to the work is huge, and I deeply appreciate them.

The great folks at Biblica have ensured that this book is far more readable and enjoyable. They have done a wonderful job and have made this a better book than it would have been without their effort.

My wife, Pamela, and my children—Jennifer (and husband Derek), Dena, Rachel, Joshua, and Harrison—are the ongoing sources of comfort, delight, and joy in my life. I am excited to see what God is doing in each of their lives as they find their place in his plan.

# CONTENTS

---

( 1 )

---

# WELCOME TO THE ADVENTURE!

God designed your spiritual life to be an adventure. Carefully, he fashioned a role for you within his great plan, a crucial place only you can fill, a special place where you alone perfectly fit. In fact, on a scale of 1 to 10, God created you to be a perfect 10 in his adventure.

When you discover where you perfectly fit, you'll also discover purpose, profound purpose—and your life will honor God. No longer will days be a series of disconnected activities that lack meaning and a primary focus. Instead, you'll live and breathe each moment aware of the *call* of God and the *plan* of God for you.

Every Christian has received a specific calling of God to ministry. So, do you know your place in God's plan? Most likely, your source of income is from a secular vocational setting. That means your primary call to ministry, your place, is within that secular setting. Your secondary call to ministry, then, is within a local church. You can view your job today—selling cars at the local dealership, processing loans at the bank, leading fitness classes at the gym—through the lens of God's call for you. This concept will bring freedom to those who view their job as a *curse* when, in reality, it is a *calling*.

Perhaps like me, your primary call is in a full-time ministry setting. If so, you and I have a secondary call to the marketplace to influence our world for Christ—as we price cars at the dealership, as we transact business at the bank, as we exercise at the local gym. It's time we stop thinking that pastors get to serve God full-time, but those in a secular job can serve God only a few hours a week. *We all serve God full-time.* Whether we work in a marketplace assignment or in a local church assignment, both are calls to ministry.

## First Steps Toward Adventure

This book is written to help you discover the specific gifts with which God has fitted you for service, the unique place God has for you in his exciting plan, and the practical resources God has provided for your use on this exciting journey. Galatians 5:13 lays the foundation for our first steps in this spiritual adventure: "You, my brothers and sisters, were called to be free. But do not use your freedom to indulge the flesh; rather, serve one another humbly in love." Called to be free. Do not use freedom to indulge the flesh. Use freedom to serve one another. But what exactly does freedom mean?

What if somehow you had complete financial freedom, beginning tomorrow morning? You might imagine taking it easy, just sauntering around in your pajamas. Maybe around ten o'clock you get dressed to go shop or play a round of golf. Then perhaps you eat out and see a movie. And when you get up the next morning, you do it all over again. You might think, *If I had total financial freedom, I would have the freedom every single day to do nothing at all.*

Sounds like freedom, right? There are, in fact, studies of people who've done exactly that. They reached retirement—finished an active, working career—and had a goal of doing nothing. Within a few years, however, many of these people died because they felt lost in the freedom of days without structure. They misunderstood the ultimate purpose of freedom: to serve, to do good things, right things, rather than doing nothing.

On the other hand, those who reach retirement and live a vital, healthy, growing, dynamic life until their last breath are the ones who say, "OK, now that I no longer have to go to that job, I get to structure my life doing things that make a difference, things that give my life purpose and meaning—whether that involves traveling or spending time with grandchildren or volunteering in my community."

I believe the freedom to do the right thing is a gift of God—and *the right thing is to serve God for his glory.* In right relationship with him, find your place of service. Come take part in a spiritual adventure that has the power to change your life. Let's begin with a process of spiritual discovery, which involves several components.

### Inquire of God

A primary component of spiritual discovery is your own individual search. As you read this book and experience the devotional materials, and as you spend time alone with God as well as in a group (see Discussion Guide at the end of this book), ask God some hard questions: "God, why did you make me the way I am? Why is it that I have these likes and dislikes? Why am I wired this way?"

### Inquire of Others

A second component of spiritual discovery is your shared experiences with others. Friends can help you see that a gift you might desire is not the one you were given.

For example, I knew a young man who believed God had called him to be a nationally known country-gospel singer. He carried a guitar and wore a cowboy hat everywhere he went. The only problem with his dream was that he couldn't sing. He did have a slight twang, but it couldn't cover up the fact that he sang every note flat. Finally, some friends said to him, "We love that you love God. We love that you want to serve him and that you're looking for a way to make an impact with your life. But, we don't think that being a country-gospel singer is God's plan for you." Because they knew him, they were able to redirect him toward goals that better fit his passion and abilities at that time. Good friends can recognize when we're working outside our giftedness.

Friends can also identify gifts within us, divinely given gifts of which we may be unaware. Friends can say to us, "You know, every time I watch you do that activity, I see God at work. Every time I hear you talk about this area, I sense the heartbeat of God in your life." The Discussion Guide at the end of this book provides material for such discussions in a group assembled for a spiritual-discovery adventure.

When we take time for both components—an individual search and a shared discovery—they become powerful mechanisms in our process of spiritual discovery.

## Spiritual DNA

In addition to your individual search and shared experiences with others, also consider in this discovery process your "spiritual DNA," that is, the spiritual forces or hardwiring within you that shape your perceptions, feelings, and behaviors. Three dimensions of your spiritual DNA must be clearly identified: your passion, gifts, and style.

### Passion

The first dimension of your spiritual DNA is *passion*—your burden, your call, your sense of "for this reason I was made." For instance, what would you feel if I talked to you about a food distribution program and about hungry people, storage issues, and distribution needs? Could you identify with that need because you know what it's like to be hungry? Would you know what it's like to have that need met by a generous person? Would your heart beat faster? Would you think, *I can do that. I can take my organizational gifts and be involved there. I have a heart for hungry people.*

Or, when you hear about a food program, perhaps you know it's not the passion God has placed in your heart. You might be more attracted to a women's outreach ministry—getting women together to learn about God's love and to care for one another. Or you're drawn to children's ministry because you see the importance of early childhood development. Maybe it's easy for you to organize things, and you feel excited about going into a church office or library or resource center and transforming chaos into order.

God wants you to serve in areas you feel passionate about. If you currently serve in an area that is not your passion, you may be on the road to burnout. You can be in a church, love God, and want to serve him—yet still become spiritually exhausted. And many times, burnout happens because people feel *obligated, responsible,* and sometimes even *guilt-tripped* into serving in areas where they have no giftedness or passion.

We all need to be willing to do things we're not necessarily passionate about. But our primary area of service should be where we feel spiritually energized. Now, just because we serve in our area of passion does not mean we won't get tired or face obstacles and struggles. Not at all. It means we may come home at the end of our ministry experience and say, "I'm tired, I'm thrashed, but God showed up, and I love doing this!"

## Gifts

The second dimension of your spiritual DNA is *gifts*. In this book, we expose you to about twenty gifts that are specifically detailed in the Bible. My own view is that the gifts listed in the Bible are not exhaustive, but illustrative. That is, the gifts that are specifically listed aren't the only spiritual gifts that exist; there may be others as well. But those listed are helpful in presenting categories of gifts so that you can more easily find the type of gifts you've been given. So God gives you not only passion, but also specific gifts in order to serve him in your areas of passion.

## Style

The third dimension of your spiritual DNA is personal *style*. This has to do with your unique personality, your distinctive way of thinking, speaking, moving, acting. Take, for example, Billy Graham. His *passion* was to see people come to know Jesus Christ as Savior and Lord. God gave Billy Graham the *gift* of evangelism. His *style* of communicating the gospel included speaking in auditoriums and stadiums filled with people. Billy Graham saw amazing things happen when he used his unique style of communicating the good news of Jesus Christ, coupled with his passion for lost people and his gift of evangelism. Whenever he spoke to a crowd and gave an invitation for people to come to know Jesus Christ, hundreds would stream out of the crowd to receive Christ as Savior, usually in the first or second verse of the hymn "Just As I Am."

What about you? You might have the passion to see people come to know Christ, and you might have the spiritual gift of evangelism, yet never in your life share Christ in front of a large group of people. You are not Billy Graham. Your passion for lost people and your gift for evangelism will play out through your personal style. You may be a quiet, gentle type, and your ministry of evangelism is praying deep, long prayers for family members and friends and coworkers. Your gentle witness in their lives plants seeds that, over time, God nurtures into a harvest. You may share Billy Graham's passion. You may share Billy Graham's gift. But because you are unique, your manner of serving God is also unique.

## Psalm 37:4

Your passion, your gift, and your personal style are linked together so that God can bring about his plan and purposes in your life. Psalm 37:4–5 tells us to

> Take delight in the LORD,
> and he will give you the desires of your heart.
>
> Commit your way to the LORD;
> trust in him and he will do this.

Take time right now to write two words on a piece of paper. First, write the word *delight;* then draw a line connecting it with the second word, *desires.* Psalm 37:4 says, "Take delight in the LORD, and he will give you the desires of your heart." I used to read that verse as saying, "If I delight myself in God, I can get anything I want." Over time as I've studied the words, I've come to believe that it is absolutely true—if I delight myself in God, he will give me the true desires of my heart.

But let me drill a bit further into these words. If I delight myself in God, he will make it so that the desires of my heart are completely fulfilled. If I learn to delight myself in God, *I will want what God wants* for my life. My highest aspiration will not be for my personal success, but instead to successfully fit into God's plan.

Now I ask you to write two other words. Write the word *commit;* then draw a line connecting it to the word *trust.* I believe that your commitment to spiritual growth is essential to fully experience God's plan for your life. For each section of this journey in *Finding Your Place in God's Plan,* an introductory lesson is followed by seven short reflections—landmarks—along the way. You can read one landmark each day to experience a six-week-long journey toward finding your place in God's plan, or you can read the landmarks over a shorter or longer period—whatever suits your style and schedule. And, gather a group of people to join you in a spiritual-discovery adventure, using the small group materials provided in the back of this book. Together, commit to discover the spiritual gifts God has given and to find a passionate way to serve him.

During this spiritual adventure, I pray that you will encounter God and that God will reveal to you why he made you the way he has. I pray that you encounter relationships with others so they can confirm the gifts God has given you or help you to reorient, if you're on the wrong path. Either way, may God use all these experiences to help you determine your perfect place in his plan.

God wants to create a radical experience in the soil of your soul so you can live celebrating his glory and honor. This spiritual adventure is all about discovering God's place for you in his plan, and I believe the results will revolutionize your world.

LANDMARK 1:
# Discover Your Unique Place

*For we are God's handiwork, created in Christ Jesus to do good works, which God prepared in advance for us to do. (Ephesians 2:10)*

Once upon a time, there was a square peg who worked in a round hole. He did his job the best he could, but he felt as if he never quite lived up to expectations. Every day, a vague emptiness hung over him, though after a while, he got used to the feeling and didn't notice it much anymore.

Once upon a time, there was a child who moved to the beat of a different drummer. It wasn't that she was rebellious.

Her ears were just tuned to music no one around her could hear. And when that music stirred her soul, she would dance jubilantly, as joy raced through her, from her toes to her outstretched fingertips. Gracious people around her would smile and shake their heads, not knowing what to do with the child. Less gracious people would interrupt the dance with a disapproving glance and a heavy hand on her shoulder. They even turned their music louder so she could hear this "more acceptable" beat—so she could exchange her dance for their ordered march. In time, she learned to step to their cadence, but people often wondered why tears ran down her face as she marched. If anyone had asked, she would have told them: the tears were the music leaking out from her heart, the music she loved and could not—would not—silence.

Once upon a time, there was a bull tromping through a china shop. As you might expect, every way he turned, something broke. He didn't mean to break things; after all, he had a sensitive heart. He was just so big and so muscular. So much power coursed through his frame that he simply couldn't keep still. Sometimes he tried to sit calmly and enjoy the beauty of the delicate things around him. But eventually, the energy inside him would build until he could no longer contain it, and he would leap and run and barrel through the store, leaving a wake of broken china behind him.

Once upon a time, you and I . . .

Some of us feel stuck in a job, in a ministry, in a life that just doesn't seem to fit us. We are square pegs stuck in a round hole. We've been there so long we've resigned ourselves to it. We've lost all hope that there might actually be a hole, the *right*-shaped hole, where *our* shape fits exactly.

Some of us feel lost in a world that neither understands nor seems to even want the gift we've been given. We move to the beat of a different drummer. Or we'd like to, if ever given the chance. In the meantime, we long to express the beauty and energy we feel inside.

Some of us feel the power of the person God made us to be. The reality of it, the energy of it, courses through our veins. But we must not be in the right place to release that power, because every time we try, we are like a bull in a china shop. Things get broken, people get hurt, and we leave pieces of our own heart behind us, strewn in a wake of jagged shards.

Sometimes, we wonder if something—or someone—could free us from this melancholy existence.

One day, the carpenter who made the square peg passed by. He saw the peg, uncomfortably stuck in a round hole. Gently, so not to break the peg, the carpenter tugged and pulled until it came free. The peg was a little scared to leave his familiar confines, but to his surprise, he also felt waves of excitement wash over him. The carpenter carried the square peg to a square hole, one made by the carpenter just for that peg. When the carpenter placed the square peg where he perfectly fit, the peg remembered hope, he discovered joy in his work, and he knew that he belonged.

It came to pass one day, as the child marched through her life, tears streaming down her face, that she met the drummer whose music she heard in her heart. When the drummer took her by the hand and danced with her, her jubilance returned. The drummer taught the girl how to keep her heart tuned to his music, how to dance strong in the midst of misunderstanding, how to dance with such winsome beauty that the scowls turned to smiles when the people heard the music themselves.

It also came to pass one day that a great lion called to the bull, through the china shop door, in a roar the bull could not refuse. The bull burst forth from the china shop and followed the lion, farther and farther, into the wild and open spaces where the bull's power and energy became forces of beauty. There, in the open spaces, he experienced freedom he'd never known. As the lion led the bull into the unexplored country, together they collected the bull's shattered dreams and transformed them into a beacon of light that penetrated the deepest recesses of others' hearts, encouraging them toward greater achievements.

Though these did not live happily ever after, they did live with richness and joy and fulfillment they had previously only dreamed of. The square peg. The child. The bull.
And you and me, if we choose to.

If you find yourself—or part of yourself—in these stories, then keep reading. You just might meet the carpenter, the drummer, the lion—the one with the power to write an unexpectedly better plot to your story. You will never be the same.

---

LANDMARK 2:
# Something to Offer

*For you created my inmost being;*
*you knit me together in my mother's womb.*
*I praise you because I am fearfully and wonderfully made;*
*your works are wonderful,*
*I know that full well. (Psalm 139:13–14)*

I once watched an interview of Meryl Streep. Widely considered among today's best American film actresses, she has remarkable versatility and range and can completely disappear into a role.

During the interview, Streep spoke fondly of playing Marian the librarian, in her high school presentation of *The Music Man.* With some coaxing from the interviewer, Streep agreed to sing a snippet of "Goodnight, My Someone," one of Marian's solos. What took place when Meryl Streep began to sing was amazing—she literally transformed before my eyes into Marian. It was remarkable to me that someone could instantaneously disappear into a role she had not played for thirty years.

In the world of theater, the world of sports, the world of business, the world of science—in any field—it's fascinating to watch those who excel at their craft. Excellence inspires us, encourages us, and calls us to reach for greater heights in our own lives.

Yes, excellence inspires us, unless that inspiration gets mired in a swamp of self-doubt and paralyzing comparison: *I'll never be that good. Why even try? I have nothing to offer.*

I don't know from whom in your life those voices might come. It could be that your parents planted those seeds in your psyche early on. Perhaps teachers or coaches or employers repeated those sentiments often enough that they echo unbidden through your mind. It might be that the enemy of your soul whispers discouragement to your heart in unguarded moments. Or maybe you've convinced yourself of your own inferiority, even in the face of encouragement from others.

Wherever those voices come from in your life, maybe it's time to listen to a new voice—to replace lying voices with the true one. What would it take for you to hear the truth loud and clear, while the lies fade to a whisper? What would it take for you to ditch the tendency to compare yourself with others who seem "better," to instead embrace the chance to prepare for the unique opportunities God created *just for you?*

What would it be like to experience the change from "I have nothing to offer—I'm a bundle of blunders," to "God created my inmost being; God knit me together in my mother's womb"?

What would it be like for "Why even try? I can't do it as well as they can" to transform into "I praise God because I am fearfully and wonderfully made; God's works are wonderful—including *me*."

May you hear God's voice affirming your value, and may you believe him when he says you have something vitally important to offer the world. When God says he designed you to be a perfect 10 in his plan for your life, may you know it, as Psalm 139 says, "full well."

## LANDMARK 3:
# Passion Quest

What are you passionate about? Chocolate ice cream? The San Francisco Giants? The environment? Children's literacy? Movies?

Specifically, what are you passionate about in ministry? Think: enthusiasm. What lights up your eyes? What stirs your gut? What fans the fire of excitement in your soul? I'll bet something does. Finding that something is your job—no one can do it for you.

Maybe you don't think of yourself as passionate; maybe you're more the stable or calm type. Just because you don't jump for joy when excited, or fly off the handle when angry, doesn't mean you're not passionate—it just means you express your enthusiasm in a quiet way.

Maybe you've never stopped to consider what you might be passionate about in ministry. That doesn't mean you're without a passion—it just means you might need to dig for it.

Maybe passion scares you; you're afraid that if you express passion for something, you might open the door for a bigger disappointment.

Stop for a moment to reflect on the stories of Scripture. God called people and shaped their ministries based on their passion. Moses had a passion to free the oppressed. Paul had a passion to reach the Gentiles for Christ. Tabitha had a passion to help the poor (Acts 9:36). Epaphras had a passion for prayer (Colossians 4:12).

Discover your passion. Acknowledge it. Release your passion. In doing so, you may find your ministry—the place God has for you.

To get started in finding your passion, ask yourself some questions.

## What Burdens Me?

Different situations and struggles affect each of us differently, in part because of our history and in part because of the unique burdens God grants to us.

For example, you might be burdened for families who've lost a child to miscarriage or death because you've also experienced such a loss. Or you may be burdened for those families simply because God laid it on your heart. Either way, that burden might indicate one passion of yours: coming alongside those suffering that kind of grief and loving them in Jesus' name.

## What Do I Dream About?

"Someday, when I take early retirement from my job, it would be so wonderful to _____." How would you fill in that blank? If money were no object, what job would you do, even if you were never paid a salary? "If I had an extra day off each week, it would be so fun to _____."

How would you inspire, help, and love people? How would you serve? What difference would you make? Analyzing what you dream about will help you uncover the passions lurking in the deep crevices of your heart.

## What Do I Feel Called to Do?

A calling to a particular profession, position, or opportunity is usually a blend of passion, gifts, and style, along with a concrete and clear sense from God's Spirit that this is what he has for you. Write on a piece of paper what you think God is calling you to do. It might be exactly what you're doing now and therefore wouldn't involve a significant job change or relocation. It might be something you've always felt was right, but you just never did it. Whatever it is, talk with a trusted Christian friend about your sense of calling and confirm it within an authentic biblical community. Then pursue it!

Your calling will probably fall strongly in line with your passions, whether you are aware of them or not.

Don't let your passion frighten you. God has shaped your heart to feel strongly and deeply about certain things, certain situations, and certain opportunities. Listen to your burdens, your dreams, and your calling; then move forward prayerfully.

---

## LANDMARK 4:
# Who Am I, Really?

When was the last time you stopped to marvel at the variety God poured into the animal kingdom—not just the diversity of appearances but also the differences in behaviors? Elephants and buffalo roam in herds; the eagle soars alone. The cheetah races like the wind; the turtle plots its every step. Lions roar; nightingales sing. Ants work in structured diligence; dolphins leap in spontaneous bursts of joy.

When was the last time you marveled at the variety God poured into the human race—the diversity of appearances as well as differences in behaviors and personalities? Marvel. Don't shake your head in bewilderment. Don't complain. Don't wonder why everyone else isn't like you—or why you're not like everyone else.

Marvel. "I praise you because I am fearfully and wonderfully made; your works are wonderful, I know that full well" (Psalm 139:14). You are fearfully and wonderfully made—body, soul, mind, and spirit. And personality, and temperament. What's more, who you are makes a difference! God made camels for the desert, whales for the ocean, falcons for the sky, and you for—well, what did he make you for? What is your natural habitat?

When considering a job offer, it's natural to compare the potential workplace with your temperament: Can I work well in a place where the phone rings constantly? Can I function well in an environment so quiet you can hear a pin drop? Would I be happy in a workplace where people constantly talk or ask me questions? Would I curl up and die in a workplace where I see only two or three people all day?

With ministry, the personality factor is no different. Think about your personality and temperament. What types of activities give you energy? What types drain you dry? There are all kinds of resources available to investigate your particular personality type. But, let's just whet your appetite; look for "you" in the following pairs of traits.

### People Oriented or Task Oriented

Those of us who are *people focused* tend to enjoy connections with other people. We're stimulated by discussions with others and by their energy. A steady stream of people and people-related issues keeps us interested and intrigued.

Those of us who are *task focused* tend to enjoy projects, with few interruptions by people. We view conversations more as tasks to accomplish something (friendship, decisions, research) rather than as a fun release. Completing tasks and reaching goals stimulate us.

Which trait best describes you? Try not to think exclusively, because people-oriented folks can be very productive, and task-oriented folks can have excellent people skills. But which area describes you most of the time?

### Unstructured or Structured

Those of us who are more *unstructured* tend to enjoy spontaneity and freedom. Daily life is free flowing rather than regimented, and we prefer working on projects in whatever order appeals to us at the moment. We rarely spend time looking at a calendar. In fact, when used, calendars are viewed as constricting and annoying necessities for living in today's world.

Those of us who are more *structured* tend to enjoy planning and are comfortable with a clearly laid out schedule. Daily routines are usually planned before they occur, borne out of efficiency and productivity goals. Entertainment and fun take place, but they are typically scheduled as any other slot of time. Calendars are critical tools, looked at several times a week—or day, or hour.

Which of the above traits best describes you? Try not to polarize the two traits: structured people can be very fun loving, and unstructured people can be on time for every appointment. But which more closely describes you? What insight does this knowledge give you into what types of ministry might fit you best?

Your God-given personality is a factor in finding a ministry that glorifies him. Don't ignore your personality when considering ways to serve God! He knitted you together, and he loves you! You are valuable.

Even if your personality traits do not reflect those typically respected in the culture around you, remember that you are a treasure—valued by the God who made you. Your fruitfulness will exponentially increase when you minister to others in a niche that fits your personality and temperament.

All of us have weak areas of our personalities we wish were stronger. Rather than focusing on those areas and working endlessly on them, focus on your areas of strength. Develop a team of people around you; include members with strengths in your areas of weakness.

Whether you are unstructured and people oriented, structured and task oriented, or some other combination, God made you and he loves you. Find out more about your unique temperament, and select serving opportunities that suit you well.

## LANDMARK 5:
# The Experience Factor

*And we know that in all things God works for the good of those who love him, who have been called according to his purpose. (Romans 8:28)*

Jazz band. High school drama. Debate team. College newspaper staff. Part-time job at an ice cream store. Paper route. Law firm internship. Cheerleading squad. Wood shop. College degree. Summers as a ranch hand. Peace Corps. The Navy. Preschool teacher. Travel. Accounting class. Auto mechanic.

When you take a look at your past, the temptation may be to see a hodgepodge of unrelated, seemingly innocuous experiences. Look harder. Look for patterns. Look for skills. Look for experiences that, when woven together, have uniquely shaped you into the person you are today. Look for the way your life experiences have uniquely prepared you to influence your world.

Foot surgery. Violence. Getting fired. Heart attack. Cancer. Mom's sudden death. Violation. Bankruptcy. Storm damage. Libel. Betrayal. Car accident. Flunking out of school. Harassment.

In all things, God works for the good of those who love him. He wants to waste nothing—not innocuous things, not ordinary things, and certainly not extraordinarily painful things. When you look at the past, the temptation may be to see a desolate field pockmarked with craters and littered with shrapnel from the physical and emotional bombs that have gone off in your life. Look harder. Don't ignore or diminish the pain of the past; instead, acknowledge the God who longs to redeem it. God is in the resurrection business, and he can resurrect something golden out of life's dull grey, no matter how painful the past. The Spirit who raised Jesus from the dead lives in you (Romans 8:11). Those brave enough to allow God to heal the wounds of their soul may find themselves uniquely equipped for effective ministry to others in pain: "Praise be to the God and Father of our Lord Jesus Christ, the Father of compassion and the God of all comfort, who comforts us in all our troubles, so that we can comfort those in any trouble with the comfort we ourselves receive from God" (2 Corinthians 1:3–4).

God can create something wonderful from your past experiences, even if they seem haphazard or unplanned. An old college degree you never used. An internship in your high school days. A hobby. A summer job. You never know how God might use your past experiences and skills training to affect his kingdom here on earth.

What you have done—and what has been done to you—can play significant roles in how you choose to serve God in the present. Begin praying now about how God might use your educational experiences, your painful experiences, your ministry experiences, and your spiritual experiences to influence the lives of others for the glory of God.

---

LANDMARK 6:

# The Desire Dilemma

*Trust in the LORD and do good;*
*dwell in the land and enjoy safe pasture.*
*Take delight in the LORD,*
*and he will give you the desires of your heart.*

*Commit your way to the LORD;*
*trust in him and he will do this:*

*He will make your righteous reward shine like the dawn,*
*your vindication like the noonday sun. (Psalm 37:3–6)*

Below is a fictional conversation between God and a person struggling with the desires of the heart. The responses I think God might
give this person are in italics. I hope this conversation helps you
understand a biblical view of your life.

> Lord Jesus,
>
> I struggle believing that you will give me the
> desires of my heart, for two reasons: I don't trust my
> heart, and I don't trust yours.
>
> *Wow. That's hard to see in black and white. But it's*
> *true, and you know my heart anyway. So is it OK if we*
> *talk about it a bit?*
>
> My first question is this: Why would you give me
> the desires of my heart? My heart is a mess—evil, hope-
> lessly fallen, tainted by sin on every level. How could
> any desire that comes from my heart be honorable or
> honored by you? You are perfect!
>
> *Have you forgotten that I'm redeeming your heart?*
>
> I guess I have. Sometimes I believe the enemy's
> lie that I'm still the person I used to be, that I'm thor-
> oughly bad, that I'm beyond fixing—that my heart
> is irreparable. Even though you are alive in me, I still
> want things I shouldn't want, do things I shouldn't do,
> think things I shouldn't think. There are still wrong
> desires lurking in me that were planted in my heart by
> my own sin and by the Devil's deceit. When I imagine
> my heart, it sometimes seems so dark. I wish you could
> show me that some of the desires I have come from
> you. I wish you could give me a better picture.
>
> *The artichoke.*

Really? The artichoke? Well, I guess that could work. Peel away the surface desires—the ones that only partly satisfy, the ones that, for all the work involved, yield only a tiny taste. Peel them all away, and get to the truest heart.

Is that it? If we could peel away the sin, the distractions, the surface wants of my heart—if we could peel all those away, would we come to the core? The part of my heart that, when redeemed, reflects what you created me to be? The part that holds the desires planted there by you—desires with pure motives that lead to your glory, others' good, and my fulfillment?

*Yes.*

But I assume you're the one who will be doing the peeling, right?

*Right. I began a good work in you, and I intend to complete it. Remember Philippians 1:6?*

But that leads to the second problem: I don't always trust your heart either. Sometimes I think your heart isn't good, that you don't really want what's best for me.

*I know.*

I'm sorry.

*We'll peel those beliefs away, too, in time. I am faithful; I am true; I am trustworthy. I died to demonstrate how much I love you—how much I want what's best for you. You know that in your mind; over time, more and more of that knowledge will trickle into the broken places of your heart. Haven't you noticed that your heart isn't nearly as messy as it used to be?*

You're right. Hope breaks through now and then—more often than it used to. I see you at work in people's lives, in my life, and I think, "Yes! Yes, it can happen—my heart is redeemed and you have planted good desires in my heart!"

Lord Jesus, keep peeling away the desires that are neither worthy of me nor of you. Redeem my desires for your purposes. Redeem my heart so that it beats to the rhythm of yours. Teach me to trust and delight in you. I look forward to seeing you fulfill the truest desires of my heart.

Amen.

LANDMARK 7:
# What If?

Finding your place in life and ministry is an exciting prospect. But sometimes the excitement comes to a halt by some persistent internal barrier. Sometimes you have to hurdle formidable mental and emotional obstacles to embrace your place in life and ministry with any measure of enthusiasm.

So, before we go any further, let's look at four barriers that might be standing in your path. Examine all of them to determine if any are present in your mind or heart. With God's help, resolve to jettison any barrier you find and press on toward your calling.

## The People Barrier

People are messy. Even at church, people are messy. They have issues. People can be territorial or immature or posers (honoring God with their lips but not their hearts). So, what happens when you *find your place* to serve and, instead of the balloons and confetti you were hoping for, instead of a crowd celebrating you fulfilling God's purpose in your life, you get no credit and grow discouraged?

It's sad, but true: sometimes things go horribly wrong. You are burned by those you serve, by co-laborers, by church leaders or pastors. So you're tempted to quit. Or you do quit, and you're now reluctant to try again.

Think about this for a minute. Yes, you have been hurt. But have you ever considered that quitting because of your hurt is a subtle form of revenge? No, you're not inflicting something harsh on the people who hurt you, but you are withholding something good from those people and even from others who just happen to be part of the same organization. So, whom are you trying to punish?

What if you actually punish yourself by holding back—keeping yourself from what you were made to do? What if you actually punish the people who would respond and grow because of your gifts? What if the best way to fight the evil and sin of the world is not by running from it, but by continuing to do good in the face of it (Romans 12:17–21)?

## The Knowledge Barrier

Maybe you would love to find your place in life and ministry, but you just don't know how. You may even fear in your heart of hearts that you are too dense to learn. Perhaps it feels as if all this spiritual stuff is written in a language you've never studied.

Don't worry. God has a habit of choosing all kinds of people—even people who have a lot to learn—to accomplish his purposes in the world (1 Corinthians 1:26–31). What if your lack of knowledge is more of a barrier for you than for God? What if God stands ready to give you the wisdom you need, if only you will ask him for it (James 1:5)?

Go ahead. Ask him. And keep reading. Keep learning. Then see what happens.

## The Schedule Barrier

This barrier is for all who believe that finding their place in life and ministry is just another item on an already-too-long to-do list. "Find my place in life and ministry!" you say. "Ha! I'd be happy just to find my living room floor." (Or the surface of my desk, the water bill, the time for lunch. You fill in the blank.)

No doubt about it. Life in our time and culture is crammed full-to-bursting with activity. And if finding your place in life and ministry sounds like yet another activity, it's likely to also sound oppressive and unappealing. You might internally argue with verses such as the one where Jesus said, "My yoke is easy and my burden is light" (Matthew 11:30).

Take a moment to think about this: What if finding your place in life and ministry doesn't mean adding one more thing to your schedule? What if it means streamlining it, peeling away things that don't match up with your heart and calling? What if it means infusing your schedule with purpose and meaning that energize rather than deplete you? What if . . . ?

Would you be willing to open a little space in your heart and your schedule to explore these "What ifs?"

## The Desire Barrier

If you listen to all the hoopla about finding your place in life and ministry, perhaps it just doesn't sound like something you want to do. You see others around you getting excited, but your heart remains unstirred by the prospect.

So many things can dampen desire: fatigue, sin, disappointment. All the barriers we've talked about can work over time to deaden your heart to its core longings for God and for the work he has prepared for you.

But what if the God who specializes in resurrections could conquer the deadness in your heart and raise that desire to life again in you? What if he would "give you a new heart and put a new spirit in you"? What if he would "remove from you your heart of stone and give you a heart of flesh" (Ezekiel 36:26)?

Would you let him?

---
2
---

# YOU'VE GOT GIFTS

I learned something about foundations when our church was being built. Meeting in temporary facilities, we desperately wanted to get into our permanent building. But it seemed to take months for the construction crew to finish laying the foundation. Really, it was only weeks, but it seemed longer, as the earth-moving equipment drove back and forth and back and forth, leveling the land and compacting the soil. I grew extremely frustrated at the pace, wondering why it was taking so long.

Then one day the foreman called us and said, "We're pouring the concrete pad for the foundation tomorrow; we'll start pouring at 3:15 in the morning." I was shocked by the early hour; nevertheless, with coffee and donuts in hand, I headed to the site early that morning to videotape the pouring of the slab. By 8:30 A.M., they had finished pouring the huge concrete slab for the foundation; then they smoothed it. But they weren't quite finished. When the slab appeared to be smooth, they shot a laser beam across the foundation from different angles, carefully and precisely making sure it was perfectly level.

At first, I didn't understand why laying the foundation took so much time. (It seemed better to me to start constructing the building itself so people could see something happening and get excited.) Then, a few weeks after the slab was poured, cranes lifted the first huge concrete panels, set them vertically, and placed them on the foundation pad. When the side panels of concrete were up, workers tied them with roof trusses and began building the roof structure above it all. As the building took shape, I realized just how much weight was resting on the soil and foundation. At that moment, I was grateful for the weeks of work spent ensuring the building's stability.

God has equipped his family with spiritual gifts. Discovering your spiritual gift will equip you to fulfill God's purpose for your life. In this chapter, we lay a general foundation for understanding spiritual gifts. Without laying the proper foundation, without making sure we have a clear perspective on the front end, we will get in trouble on the back end.

## 1 Corinthians 12

When trying to understand a topic, it's sometimes good to review the Bible from cover to cover to see what it says about that topic. Other times, we can go to one particular section of Scripture to find a key teaching on it. For instance, if we want to know about the tenderness of God, we might go to Psalm 23 to read the Shepherd's Psalm, which describes the character of the heart of God and the tenderness with which he loves us (as a shepherd cares for his sheep). If we want to think about the love of God and the character and nature of that love, we might go to 1 Corinthians 13—called the Love Chapter because it contains a beautiful, poetic, powerful description of love.

While many passages in the New Testament talk about spiritual gifts, the key passage is 1 Corinthians 12. In the first verse of 1

Corinthians 12, we are told this: "Now about the gifts of the Spirit, brothers and sisters, I do not want you to be uninformed." God wants to draw our attention to this topic, to inform us. If we love Jesus and want to fulfill God's purpose in our lives, we need to pay attention to this text about spiritual gifts. Spiritual gifts are foundational to our spiritual lives.

Then, in 1 Corinthians 12:4–6, we read, "There are different kinds of gifts, but the same Spirit distributes them. There are different kinds of service, but the same Lord. There are different kinds of working, but in all of them and in everyone it is the same God at work." Let's examine what these verses mean.

## It's All about the Giver

First, verse 4 says there are different kinds of gifts, but the same Spirit. There is only one Spirit—who distributes spiritual gifts to believers. Second, verse 5 says there are different kinds of service, but the same Lord. Service refers to ministries in which the gifts are used. Third, verse 6 tells us there are different kinds of working— that is, effects or impacts—but the same God. In other words, using a gift in a ministry will have an impact, but there is only one Spirit, or one God, who works all these things together.

So, if there are different gifts but one Spirit, different ministries but one Lord, and different effects but only one God, then what does the working of spiritual gifts and the impact of all that have to do with me, with my worth or value? *Absolutely nothing!* If when focusing on the topic of spiritual gifts we find ourselves looking at the *individual* who is the recipient of the gift or looking at the *impact* or *outworking* of the gift, instead of looking at the God who gave the gift, then we are "catawampus to the world."

The reality is that the gifts, the ministries, and the effects are all about the Father, the Son, and the Holy Spirit—*not about us.* If we do not get that straight, we will get catawampus to the world. We will get it all confused if we focus on the effect of the gift or on the person who has the gift—and we will lose our focus on God.

Let me give a couple of illustrations. Let's say that you think you have the gift of exhortation, which is the gift of building up or challenging people to grow further in their relationship with God. Let's say you want to exercise that gift in singing, because God also gave you a powerful voice. So, you study, prepare, and plan. Your dream is to use your gift in a stadium so you could minister as a solo artist to thousands of people. But, instead of that opportunity presenting itself, you're asked to lead the singing in a small group of twelve people, six who sing off key. If you don't understand gifts and ministries and effects, you might get angry about that "lesser" opportunity.

Or, let's say your gift is teaching; your dream is to teach in a small-group setting. So, you prepare for that ministry and an opportunity arrives. But instead of a small group of twelve or so, only two people show up. And they're barely awake through the whole class.

*Only when we understand that gifts and ministries and effects are about God will we be at peace with our assignment from God.* Spiritual gifts come from God, ministry opportunities are assigned by God, and the effects are ultimately up to God. We can only be open to an assignment when we are at peace with the fact that it is God who distributes the gift, God who assigns the ministry, and God who decides the outworking of it all. Serving God is about God. It is not about us.

Let me give a very personal application. Before founding a church in Carson Valley, Nevada (www.cvcwired.com), I served at the denominational level. As I traveled to various places for that role, I saw ministry leaders who had reached the end of their public ministry life, and their teaching effectiveness had clearly diminished. They were on the downhill slope of their ability to effectively communicate God's Word. I was frightened enough by that prospect in my own ministry that I actually told my wife if ever she saw that my abilities were diminished, I wanted her to plainly let me know so I could get out of the public role and serve somewhere else.

I've also articulated those thoughts to my church family. This is a way for me to be accountable for my gifts, and I would want nothing less for my church. My prayer is that I will have the spiritual maturity to serve in a different capacity for the sake of the kingdom of God when this assignment is over and I enter a different season of my life.

## Given to Each, Used for All

First Corinthians 12:7 gives another interesting foundational truth about spiritual gifts: "Now to each one the manifestation of the Spirit is given for the common good." That tells us that every Christ-follower has at least one spiritual gift. That's worth celebrating!

In our home, we've had the experience of inviting people over to celebrate Christmas and discovering to our horror that, at the last minute, somebody had come for whom we didn't have a gift. It's an awkward situation, to say the least. In our house, that experience throws us into a panic, and immediately my wife has to find and wrap a gift.

Spiritual life is not a party where somebody comes and leaves without a gift. If you are a Christ-follower, you are at the table and a gift is prepared for you. I'm convinced, however, that many of us go through the journey of life with wrapped gifts that remain unopened. Romans 12:4–5 says, "Just as each of us has one body with many members, and these members do not all have the same function, so in Christ we, though many, form one body, and each member belongs to all the others." The truth is that God has a place for you in his plan, and this place is matched with your spiritual gift. You must open and understand the gift he has given you and put it into play.

## Use Your Gift Well

A number of years ago, I came across some observations of A. T. Pierson regarding spiritual gifts. (Find A. T. Pierson's list in *The 33 Laws of Stewardship* by Dave Sutherland and Kirk Nowery, Spire Resources, 2003.) I've found these seven points to be helpful, and I share them with you in a somewhat adapted form.

1. *Every believer has at least one gift, so everyone should be encouraged.* Everybody who is a Christ-follower receives at least one gift. You should be encouraged because you were invited to the party, and God has a gift for you!

2. *No one has all the gifts, so everyone should be humble.* Jesus was the only one to walk the face of the earth perfectly equipped to do every job description in the kingdom. So, since you don't have all the gifts—and neither do I—we need the gifts of other people to complement our own. This should help keep us humble.

3. *All the gifts are for Christ's work; so all work should be harmonious.* If we start to focus only on the project at hand, or on each other, or on our conflicts, we will lose the harmony we should be pursuing. Since our gifts are for the work of Jesus, keeping our eyes on him will help build unity where disunity would be natural. We need to remember that we are all working for the same boss.

4. *All gifts are to be used for Christ's glory, so everyone should be content.* This is really challenging. Every once in a while, we see Christians who, because of their spiritual gifts, have an attitude of superiority over other Christians. In other words, they elevate themselves, thinking their gifts are more important than those of others. How foolish to use our gifts as an excuse for pride. We have nothing that we did not receive by grace and for the glory of God.

5. *All gifts are to build up the body of Christ, so everyone should be mutually helpful.* We need to be careful how we use our gifts. We should never use them in ways that bring destruction or defeat or discouragement. We should be careful to build up one another in Christ so that the body matures.

6. *All gifts are for spiritual health, so they all are necessary.* God designed the gifts and God distributes them as he sees fit. We need all the spiritual gifts. They all work together for the spiritual health of the spiritual community.

7. *All gifts require God's Spirit at work, so we should be spiritually in tune.* If we want to use the gifts God has entrusted to the church in ways that give God glory and honor and that fulfill his purpose for our individual lives and for the church in the world, we have to walk in the light of God's Word and in the power and rhythm of the indwelling Holy Spirit.

Let me tell you a mistake I made earlier in my Christian life. When I watched somebody who had an obvious gift of God, I would jump to the wrong conclusion. I would see the ministry that person had been assigned and the obvious effect of that gift on others, and I would assume that he or she was a spiritually mature person.

I want to be clear on this point: *It is possible for a person to have a spiritual gift, be assigned to ministry, and for a time see powerful effects; yet that person can still be self-centered, flesh-driven, and ambitious for personal good and glory.* When immature people have a positive impact, that is a testimony to the grace and power of God to use flawed and failing vessels for his glory and honor.

Spiritual gifts and ministries and effects have nothing to do with spiritual maturity. They have to do with how God has chosen to work in the world. Sometimes God entrusts great gifts to immature people and gives them opportunities to do ministry and produce wonderful effects. Tragically, the results can also be disastrous. If we are not depending on God throughout the process of doing ministry, we too will eventually go off in the ditch, taking a host of people with us.

The televangelist scandals in the mid-1980s were a formative influence in my life. I observed a number of people whom God had clearly entrusted with powerful gifts. He had given them huge ministry opportunities, and he had caused tremendous, positive effects. Some of those ministers, however, started thinking it was all about their personal power and glory and not about God's. We must be careful to humbly avoid the pride that leads to destruction. The gifts of God are powerful, and we must exercise meek caution. We must use them exclusively to glorify God, not ourselves.

## Go Ahead, Open It

There are two questions I want to ask you at this point in our journey:

1. Will you commit to discover the spiritual gift God has given you? God longs for you to discover all the gifts he has for you. You do have an enemy of your soul who wants you to remain ignorant of God's gifts and dream for your life. Will you turn to God for the courage to discover the gift(s) he has given you?

2. Will you use your gift for God's team? God has a place for you, and I don't know where that place is. Many of you will discover that your place is not within the four walls of a church, but rather is outside, in another part of the community. Wherever your place of ministry, remember you are building the kingdom of God, not your own kingdom.

God has assigned each of us a strategic web of relationships. Right now you have the opportunity to influence several people for Jesus Christ. Many of you have been intentionally placed in a context where people know nothing about the Bible, nothing about Jesus, and nothing about church—except for what they see and hear in you. Will you discover the gift that God has given you, and will you find your place on God's team? If you do, you will discover that life is an adventure and that God has given you the tools to navigate the course and be successful on the journey of life.

LANDMARK 8:
# Spiritual Gifts 101

God has given you spiritual gifts. Discovering your spiritual gifts equips you to fulfill God's purpose for your life.

> *There are different kinds of gifts, but the same Spirit distributes them. There are different kinds of service, but the same Lord. There are different kinds of working, but in all of them and in everyone it is the same God at work. Now to each one the manifestation of the Spirit is given for the common good. (1 Corinthians 12:4–7)*

There are terms in the Christian faith that, at first glance, seem mysterious and difficult to understand: *sanctification, atonement, fruit of the Spirit, Last Supper.* Then there is the term *spiritual gifts.* Mysterious. Puzzling. Controversial. We might want to ignore such mysterious terms and focus on other, more clear aspects of the faith. But there is a verse in the Bible that won't let us do that: "Now about the gifts of the Spirit, brothers and sisters, I do not want you to be uninformed" (1 Corinthians 12:1).

So much for the ignorance-is-bliss approach to faith. God doesn't want spiritual gifts to be a mysterious, unapproachable topic. In fact, God sees spiritual gifts as a key component in the way we relate to each other and to the world.

So, what do we need to know? Leave the controversy for a different time! We'll just deal with the basics for now. First, let's get a definition: *Spiritual gifts are special capacities the Holy Spirit gives to believers to enable them to do God's work in the church and in the world.* The following are some core truths about spiritual gifts. Read them a couple of times, and look up the verses referenced.

- Spiritual gifts are just that—gifts. You don't earn them or choose them; you receive them (1 Corinthians 12:11).
- God gives every believer—that includes you and me—one or more spiritual gifts (1 Corinthians 12:7; Ephesians 4:7).
- God gifted you for a purpose (Ephesians 4:11–13).
- God gifted you for his people (1 Peter 4:10; 1 Corinthians 12:7; Romans 12:4–5).

Those are the basics. We'll examine these basics further so that we can all avoid ignorance about this key component in the community of faith.

---

LANDMARK 9:
# "Grace" Gifts

*(Scene: Billy's front yard. Billy is dancing around, showing off a shiny new toy, singing about it to his friend Sam.)*

BILLY: I'm so great! Look at me! I have the toy of the century!

SAM: That's a great toy. You got it for your birthday, right?

BILLY: No. I've always had it!

SAM: No way. Your dad gave it to you. I saw him!

BILLY: You're just jealous 'cuz you don't have one too! You're just jealous that I'm better than you!

SAM: Yeah, right. *(Shakes his head and exits, leaving Billy to dance alone.)*

Sounds silly, doesn't it? This kind of scene causes us wiser, more mature people to shake our heads at the folly of youth. Billy has a great toy, but he wasn't born with it. His loving dad gave it to him. How immature of Billy to think that his birthday present makes him better than his friend Sam! Good thing we've all grown out of that behavior.

Or have we?

Grace is a key theme in the Christian faith. Grace means that I get something I need but don't deserve; I get it not by earning it, but as a gift. I don't deserve salvation, but by God's grace and his gift of Jesus, I have it. I don't deserve forgiveness, but by God's grace, I receive it. I know my internal propensity to stray from God; because of that, I must rely on grace moment by moment.

When it comes to gifts, however, sometimes we leave the grace theme behind. Grace isn't necessarily the first thing that comes to mind when we think about our spiritual gifts. We may even say the words "our spiritual gifts" with the emphasis on "our" rather than on "gifts." Sometimes we are so recognized in the church for our gifts and abilities that we forget the gifts are a "God thing," not an "us thing." It is by grace alone that we receive our gifts.

In fact, the New Testament word usually translated "spiritual gift" is *charismata,* a Greek word from the root *charis,* meaning "grace." Some churches even refer to spiritual gifts as "grace gifts" to enhance the true meaning of the term. We are gifted by grace.

When we forget that truth, we start sounding like young Billy. We sound as if we have earned the gifts or chosen the gifts, as though we possessed the gifts inherently. We show off, we boast, we take credit for something we had no part in. Silly, isn't it? Believers have great spiritual gifts, but we weren't born with them. Our loving Father gave them to us through his Holy Spirit. He picked them out and distributed them as he chose. How immature of us to take credit for them or to think that our particular gift makes us better than our friends! When do you suppose we will grow out of that sort of behavior?

The next time you receive recognition for your spiritual gift, watch your reaction. Receiving the compliment *gracefully* may mean just that: giving credit to God's *grace* for his work in your life.

# To Err Is Human

To err is human, we say. And we're right.

When I'm told that God has placed in every believer a spiritual gift or gifts, I tend to err in one of two directions. Each of these extremes prevents God from working in and through me to the extent he would like. In any given week, I can travel from one error to the other and back again on a round-trip ticket.

Some days God says to me, "I've given you a gift," and I think he has made an unwise choice.

Why? Because I know myself pretty well. I know that I'm capable of bad stuff. When I take a close look at the grossest evils committed by people during the past century, a hard truth emerges: the perpetrators were not as far from "normal" as I would like to think. Because of the darkness in my own heart, I know that I'm capable of choices under certain circumstances that are horribly evil.

*So why in the world would God put a spiritual gift in me? How could I be worthy of such a treasure? I can understand why he would give me something corresponding to what I deserve, but why a gift that's good? In grace? It just doesn't add up.*

Other days God says to me, "I've given you a gift," and I think he has made a very wise choice.

Why? Because I know myself pretty well. I know that I am capable of great stuff. When I look at the people throughout history who have accomplished the greatest feats, I see that many of them started off as I did! I can do it: effective decision making, strategic thinking, decisive leadership, loyal friendship, kind parenting, authentic service to God.

*Of course God has placed spiritual gifts in me! Look at me—I'm on top of the world! In fact, I'm worthy of even more treasure. God should have given me more gifts, because I would have used them in awesome, effective ways.*

To err is human, we say. And we're right. When God tells me he has given me a gift, I tend to err in one of two directions— either into the morass of self-loathing or into the trap of self-sufficiency.

The reality is that God did give to me a gift. To me. And he gave it with full awareness of my weaknesses and my strengths. I don't need to emphasize—or deny—either of them. I don't have to fear that my weaknesses are bigger than God's ability to use me—or feel the need to cover up or fix my weaknesses *before* God can use me. My strengths will never enable me to function apart from God; but, conversely, there is no need to cover up my strengths and create a false dependence or false humility.

To err is human. But to learn is human, too. So today when God says to me, "I've given you a gift," instead of saying, "You shouldn't have" or "Of course you have," I would like to learn to say "Thank you."

# How to Spot a Gift at Work

Maybe you feel that you wouldn't know a spiritual gift if it jumped up and bit you. But maybe you would get better at spotting spiritual gifts at work if you began asking the right sort of questions. Here are a few to get you started.

## Part 1: Recognizing Gifts in Others

- Think of a time when God put a believer in your life who served as a catalyst for you to grow in your faith. Who was that person?
- Describe that person. What was it about his or her character that drew you in? What qualities, experiences, and abilities do you think God placed in that person that made him or her especially able to help you?
- How did you grow in your faith because of your time with that person?
- Spend a few minutes thanking God for the gift of that person in your life.

During your time with that person, you probably weren't thinking about spiritual gifts. But if you indeed grew in your faith, it was in part because he or she utilized the spiritual gifts of God.

## Part 2: Recognizing Gifts in Yourself

- Now, if you are a believer, think of a time when God placed you in someone's life to be a catalyst for that person to grow in faith. Who was that person?
- What was it about your character that drew that person to you? What qualities, experiences, and abilities do you

think God placed in you that made you especially able to help that person?

- How did that person grow in his or her faith because of your time together?
- Spend a few minutes thanking God for what he did through you and in that person's life.

During your time with that person, you probably weren't thinking about spiritual gifts. But if that person grew in his or her faith, you were utilizing the spiritual gifts of God.

# Once upon an Eternity

Once upon an eternity, an angel approached God in his workshop. The Father was brushing dust off his hands and humming to himself as he put away his tools.

"What are you making?" asked the angel.

God smiled. "Take a look," he said, nodding toward the corner of his workshop.

The angel looked to see a human being, a female, with wavy, dark hair and a shining intelligence that burned from her amber eyes. She had a quick smile and a graceful bearing. She swayed contentedly to the rhythm of the music that pulsed through the very air of heaven. The angel felt his heart leap. He never grew tired of witnessing his Creator's latest work.

"What will *she* do?" the angel whispered. "Which of your mighty purposes will she work to fulfill?"

"Hmmm," God mumbled, his brow furrowing in momentary puzzlement, "I don't know." The Father shrugged and gave his angel a bemused smile. "I just felt like puttering around for a while in the workshop, and I had a few spare parts lying around."

Whoa! Time out! Something just went terribly wrong with the plotline. God is not an absent-minded artist, doodling aimlessly on the canvas of the universe. When he creates something, he has a reason for it, a purpose for its existence. Every person, every mountain, every moment, every gift has its place in the cosmos and its role in the mighty purposes of God.

Hear this: you have a purpose. There is a reason God created you. You are not a collection of spare parts swept up from the Father's workshop floor. The gifts you have are not yours by chance—the result of some heavenly lottery. The Holy Spirit of God specifically chose those gifts to plant within you to accomplish eternal purposes: to touch lives, to build the church, to advance the kingdom, to defeat the enemy. God gave you gifts because he has something he wants you to do with them. Remember: "For we are God's handiwork, created in Christ Jesus to do good works, which God prepared in advance for us to do" (Ephesians 2:10).

If we lead an aimless, wandering existence, it is not for lack of vision on God's part. If we want someone to blame, let's acknowledge our own tendency to let the trivia of life eclipse the purpose of life, our own propensity to believe the enemy's lie that our existence is meaningless. God is here with us, breathing purpose into our days—working in us, as Paul wrote, "to will and to act in order to fulfill his good purpose" (Philippians 2:13).

Let's strike a blow against the enemy and strive to uncover God's eternal purpose for us—and pursue it with passion and diligence: "In a large house there are articles not only of gold and silver, but also of wood and clay; some are for special purposes and some for common use. Those who cleanse themselves from the latter will be instruments for special purposes, made holy, useful to the Master and prepared to do any good work" (2 Timothy 2:20–21).

Let's make it our goal to be prepared for any good work God has prepared for us—"to take hold of that for which Christ Jesus took hold of me" (Philippians 3:12). Let's try to serve God's purpose in our generation, as David did in his (Acts 13:36).

Let's take another look at the heavenly scene unfolding.

"What will *she* do?" the angel whispered. "Which of your mighty purposes will she work to fulfill?"

"Ah," God smiled, his face awash with delighted anticipation. "Sit down, angel. Let me tell you about the wondrous gifts I have planted in this one, the works I have prepared for her to do. Listen . . ."

LANDMARK 13:
# The Inheritance

Jean was well into her twenties when she got a phone call from the family attorney: At the age of ninety-four, Aunt Betty had died, and Jean was the sole heir to her estate.

Jean felt she hadn't known her great aunt well. Aunt Betty preferred to keep to herself most of the time, except for the annual Twelfth Night dinner she hosted each year for the entire family. Through the years of Twelfth Night celebrations, Jean had made an effort to ask about and tend to simple repairs needed around her aunt's house. Once, Jean had genuinely complimented the home's architecture and spoke well of it to her aunt.

She had hardly meant to finagle an inheritance by making the repairs or giving the compliment, but, now that it had happened, Jean relished the idea of owning her aunt's home. It actually suited Jean nicely in both style and location. The house was old and needed a lot of work, but it was owned free and clear. There were no other known assets—no automobiles, no retirement accounts, nothing. It appeared that Aunt Betty had lived off Social Security and her gardens. Jean knew her aunt was not a woman of wealth, but it did surprise her that Aunt Betty didn't even have a checking account.

After moving in, Jean took some time each weekend to make the home her own. She replaced some decorations and old photos, and when spring came, she even managed to plant a small vegetable garden in the yard.

Jean, however, consistently avoided one room: the library. Its walls were lined with books as well as every issue of *National Geographic* ever printed. Most of the books were paperbacks and appeared to have been published within the past forty years or so. Prices written in pencil on the inside covers ranged from twenty-five to fifty cents, suggesting to Jean that Aunt Betty would visit garage sales to collect as many paperback books as she could read in a given week. To a non-reader such as Jean, the library was a wasted room: dusty, musty, and boring. She usually kept the door shut.

Over the next few years, Jean took on various remodeling and redecorating projects. The house looked great and became a favorite gathering spot for Jean's friends. During the summer months, Jean would often have friends over for barbeques, impressing them with her homegrown vegetables and her remodeling skills. During one dinner, Paul, one of Jean's friends, found the library and took interest in a book. When he left that night, he asked Jean if he could borrow it. "I've never read this particular Ludlum book. May I keep it for a week or so?" Jean shrugged her okay—it made no difference to her.

The oddest thing happened when Jean saw Paul at church the next weekend. "May I keep the book?" Paul asked excitedly. Jean wasn't sure how to read Paul's emotion, so she didn't answer right away. But Paul laughed and said, "Just kidding! It's in my car. I'll go get it." When Paul handed Jean the book, he said, "I'll bet your aunt paid a lot of money for that book!" Before Jean could respond, Paul was interrupted and turned to speak with someone else.

At home, Jean absent-mindedly flipped through the pages of the book. As she did so, a one-hundred-dollar bill fell to the floor! Paul had put a sticky note over Ben Franklin's face with this note: "This is the costliest bookmark I've ever used!" Jean was confused. Why would Paul give Jean money? Jean had given Paul a loan a few months before, but he paid it back. Paul had worked on Jean's car, but Jean paid him the day of the repair. It all seemed so odd.

That night, Jean picked up the book on her way to bed, thinking she might try reading it. But she read only half of the first chapter when she set the book down and turned off the light. The money still confused Jean. *Why would Paul pay her $100? And why would he suggest that Aunt Betty had paid a lot for the book? She had probably paid only fifty cents for it.*

Suddenly, Jean bolted upright in bed and gasped. *Aunt Betty must have put the money in the book!* Jean gasped again, ran to the library, and began pulling a row of paperbacks off a shelf. As she threw them to the floor, money fell out—a lot of money—$1,500 from that shelf alone. Some books held $100, others $200, but most had $300 or $400. The library had been Aunt Betty's bank! Over the years she had squirreled away an entire life's savings in those books and magazines. Jean stayed up all night counting and stacking money (and, she checked the lock on her front door twice during the night). When she finally finished looking through every book and magazine twice, she had counted $318,700 in cash. Aunt Betty wasn't poor; she was frugal! And she had left it all to Jean.

Inheriting an older house in the country was generous, a helpful start for Jean to build on and improve. Receiving over $300,000 in cash was overwhelming to her. She called in sick that day and slept fitfully all morning. *What should I do?* she wondered. And she punished herself all morning for hating books, for avoiding the library, for barely looking in there during the three years she had lived in the house.

"If I had only known that money was hidden in the house, I would have looked!" she shouted.

Sometimes we toss aside a treasure, mistaking it for trash. We're prone to dismiss as nonsense the inner nudge that could lead us to something truly valuable. All too often, we are blind to the riches sitting right under our nose.

No wonder the apostle Paul prayed like this: "I pray that the eyes of your heart may be enlightened in order that you may know the hope to which he has called you, the riches of his glorious inheritance in his holy people, and his incomparably great power for us who believe" (Ephesians 1:18–19).

If you knew that God has an inheritance for you, wouldn't you look for it? If you knew you had access to spiritual *riches,* wouldn't you search for them?

## REST STOP!

Spend some time in prayer today. Ask God to help you make sense of what you've learned so far. Ask him to help you maintain stamina and excitement for the rest of this spiritual adventure!

# 3

# MAKING SENSE
# OF THE MOSAIC

I enjoyed the movie *Cast Away*. In it, Tom Hanks plays a FedEx executive who is on a plane making last-minute Christmas deliveries. The plane crashes in the Pacific Ocean, and Hanks' character floats to an uninhabited island, where he is stranded for five years. During this time, he leaves one package that he had salvaged from the wreck unopened, so he can deliver it if he's ever rescued.

FedEx, during Superbowl XXXVII, actually ran a commercial spoofing the film. An actor who looks like Hanks has been rescued from the island. He shows up at the address written on the unopened package to be greeted by the lady of the house. He tells the woman he had been marooned on an island for five years with the package and that he'd sworn to deliver it to her—because he works for FedEx. He hands her the package, she takes it, and thanking him, she begins to close the door.

He curiously asks, "By the way, what's in the package?"

She opens it and says, "Nothing really, just a satellite phone, GPS locator, fishing rod, water purifier, and some seeds."

That's the way some of us live. We possess packages that contain exactly what we need. There are treasures right in front of our noses, and we don't even see them. This spiritual adventure is about you finding your place in God's plan and opening the treasure he has entrusted to you. Your treasure is your spiritual gift. If you're unaware of it, it is an unopened package that contains exactly what you need to find your place in God's plan.

In the previous chapter, we learned that God gives to all believers in Christ a spiritual gift, that is, a tool that equips us to do his work in his kingdom, and in this way to fulfill his purpose for our lives and for his world.

In the New Testament, four primary books address spiritual gifts. We've spent a lot of time in one of them, 1 Corinthians 12; in this chapter, we continue there and go a little deeper.

First Corinthians 12:7–11 says this:

> Now to each one [that means every person who is a Christ-follower] the manifestation of the Spirit is given for the common good. To one there is given through the Spirit a message of wisdom, to another a message of knowledge by means of the same Spirit, to another faith by the same Spirit, to another gifts of healing by that one Spirit, to another miraculous powers, to another prophecy, to another distinguishing between spirits, to another speaking in different kinds of tongues, and to still another the interpretation of tongues. All these are the work of one and the same Spirit, and he distributes them to each one, just as he determines.

As we've learned, all spiritual gifts are given for the common good. The gifts are given to equip us to do God's will, to grow God's family, to see God work in our lives, and to glorify God.

We've also learned that if our focus ever becomes the gifts or the ministry or the effect of the gifts, then we have strayed off-course.

The focus of the gifts is to remain on God alone. We get excited about gifts. But God wants us to focus on him, the *giver*, not on the gifts.

Continuing in 1 Corinthians 12, another key passage on gifts is found in verses 28–30.

> God has placed in the church first of all apostles, second prophets, third teachers, then miracles, then gifts of healing, of helping, of guidance, and of different kinds of tongues. Are all apostles? Are all prophets? Are all teachers? Do all work miracles? Do all have gifts of healing? Do all speak in tongues? Do all interpret?

All of those questions are rhetorical, and each expects a negative answer: no, not everyone works miracles, not everyone has gifts of leadership, not everyone has gifts of mercy, not everyone speaks in tongues. So, Paul was saying to earnestly desire the greater gifts. The first part of the passage talks about apostles, prophets, evangelists, pastors, and teachers. Some believe these are not spiritual gifts, but rather offices in the church. Reasonable Christians can disagree on this point. My position is that while these are offices in the church, they also require specific gifts. In other words, I think the office of apostle requires the gift of apostleship; the office of teacher requires the gift of teaching. It makes sense that they are not solely offices, but also gifts that equip those offices.

Romans 12:6–8 is another important passage on the topic of spiritual gifts.

> We have different gifts, according to the grace given to each of us. If your gift is prophesying, then prophesy in accordance with your faith; if it is serving, then serve; if it is teaching, then teach; if it is to encourage, then give encouragment; if it is giving, then give generously; if it is to lead, do it diligently; if it is to show mercy, do it cheerfully.

There are two final passages we will review. Ephesians 4:11 says, "So Christ himself gave the apostles, the prophets, the evangelists, the pastors and teachers . . ." And 1 Peter 4:9–10 says, "Offer hospitality to one another without grumbling. Each of you should use whatever gift you have received to serve others."

Wait a minute—offer hospitality? What does that have to do with spiritual gifts? Verse 9 says, "Offer hospitality," and verse 10 says, "Use whatever gift you have." In the Greek text, those form one sentence. So most people connect verse 9 with verse 10 and say that hospitality is actually a gifting of God. Some people have a supernatural ability to encourage others by making them feel warmly welcomed.

> Each of you should use whatever gift you have received to serve others, as faithful stewards of God's grace in its various forms. If anyone speaks, they should do so as one who speaks the very words of God. If anyone serves, they should do so with the strength God provides, so that in all things God may be praised through Jesus Christ. To him be the glory and the power for ever and ever. Amen. (1 Peter 4:10–11)

If you go through those five passages and make a list of the different gifts, eliminating duplicates, you will have somewhere between nineteen and twenty-one spiritual gifts. I think these listings are illustrative, rather than exhaustive. That is, they are perhaps a general list of gifts that do not limit God's creativity in uniquely gifting every believer for some particular service in the body of Christ. Let's group these gifts into ministry categories as one way of organizing them.

## Ministry Growth Gifts

The first category of gifts we will consider is ministry growth gifts. These are gifts useful in establishing new churches and in developing and growing them.

The first ministry growth gift is *apostleship:* the ability to extend God's ministry into unreached areas and influence movements of people. I think some missionaries use the apostolic gift as they travel into unreached territories. God calls them into areas where the gospel, the good news of Jesus, has never been preached (the word *apostle* means "one sent forth").

I also think there are people with apostolic gifts who have influence and authority over a movement. For example, in the book of Acts, we see the apostles, who experienced the living Christ face to face, exercise unique leadership in the early church movement. And not only then, but the gift of apostleship—extending the gospel to unreached areas and having influence over movements—is still very real and very important to the mission of the church today.

The second ministry growth gift is *prophecy:* declaring with power the word of God. Some people think that prophets only foretold future events. Not at all. Most of the time, the biblical prophets weren't "foretelling" the future, but rather they were "forthtelling" the truth of God to the nation of Israel. They were speaking words God gave them to inform Israel about the consequences of obeying and disobeying the laws of God spelled out in their covenant with him. Once again, this is not a gift to be handled lightly. Biblical prophecy came directly from God, and it was infallible. If someone claimed to be a prophet of God but one of his prophecies proved false, he was stoned to death. A true prophet of God is always accurate because he is quoting God's words.

I believe that I have the gift of teaching, but not the gift of prophecy. However, there have been times when, in communicating God's Word, I could feel the Spirit of God take over. The words that came out of my mouth and the ways in which God's Spirit penetrated people's hearts caused me to realize that my anointed preparation and my careful deliberation had nothing to do with the effects. The Spirit of God was working in a prophetic, forthtelling manner to proclaim the words of God with power to change people's hearts.

The third ministry growth gift is *pastoring:* shepherding other believers to spiritual maturity. Some of you will never serve in the office of pastor, yet you have a pastoring or shepherding gift, a call to be a spiritual mentor of others. These people have a gifting to help others grow in their faith, from infancy to maturity.

The fourth ministry growth gift is *teaching:* communicating God's Word with effectiveness to believers and to unbelievers. John Stott, when elaborating on the famous saying of theologian Karl Barth, said that the goal of the communicator, the teacher of God's Word, is to take the newspaper in one hand, God's Word in the other, and build a bridge between the two, so that the timeless truth of God's Word connects with the reality of today's news. A person with a teaching gift can tell us what God's Word says and how it relates to our daily lives.

The fifth ministry growth gift is *evangelism:* sharing the gospel so that people are reached for Christ. My dad had the gift of evangelism. He enjoyed witnessing for Christ in restaurants, at gas stations, and especially on airplanes (because, where are people going to go?). We kids often felt embarrassed during those times. Over the last ten years of his life, he would hang out at the local donut shop with his WWII buddies. At my dad's funeral service, about fifteen people talked about the effect my dad had in sharing his faith at the donut shop. Some of them were believers in Christ; others had not yet committed their lives to Christ. But out of respect for the impact he had on them, they came to the memorial service. We believe those evangelism talks at the donut shop will result in expanding the kingdom of heaven.

The sixth ministry growth gift is *leadership:* the God-given ability to envision God's future and equip people to get there. Paraphrasing one of George Bernard Shaw's characters, Robert F. Kennedy said, "There are those that look at things the way they are, and ask *why?* I dream of things that never were, and ask *why not?*" In the church, there are people who have the ability to see the future, seize it, and bring it into the present. If you've been around people with a leadership gift, you no doubt heard them describe the future. Theirs is not the fanciful description of some ungrounded dreamer, but a vision from God about where to go.

All these gifts equip and enable the body of Christ to go where God is leading, fulfilling his vision for his church.

## Ministry Support Gifts

Those with ministry support gifts serve in support roles for the body of Christ.

The gift of *administration* includes mobilizing and galvanizing God's people to accomplish God's purposes. I always thought the gift of administration was the ability to move paper from one side of the desk to another. What I've discovered over time is that the gift of administration is vital, especially for a large church. Last Sunday, we had almost three hundred children on our church campus during five services, and to my knowledge, there were no fatal accidents. All of the classes were supplied with the necessary resources for teaching, crafts, snacks, and music. You can be assured some administratively gifted people in our children's ministry are running things behind the scenes, making sure the in-class ministry folks have whatever they need to touch a child's heart.

The gift of *helps* is serving in a capacity to ensure that ministry happens wherever, whenever. I love people with the gift of helps, because they don't care who gets the credit. They don't care what's going on; they are just willing to do whatever it takes to help out.

When we were starting our church, I prayed that God would first send people with the gift of giving (I won't lie—we really needed generous givers in those days) and people with the gift of helps. We needed a lot of help. Every single week we had to set up and tear down; we used carts to move things in and out of temporary locations, starting at 6:30 on Sunday mornings. You have to be a person with the gift of helps to be willing to do all of that behind-the-scenes activity! Every week at our church, people with this gift serve donuts, hand out programs, wipe noses in children's classes. They're willing to do whatever it takes to abundantly serve those who come.

Believers equipped with the gift of *exhortation* encourage and admonish others toward spiritual maturity. The Pauline Epistles in the New Testament are full of exhortation and encouragement. We see this gift in Paul's life when we read about his heartbeat for the churches he had planted throughout his ministry. When we speak to one another in love, we build each other in our faith; those who have this gift see God use them to strengthen other believers (Ephesians 4:25–32).

The gift of *giving* is the supernatural capacity (and accompanying joy) to give generously in areas of time, talent, and treasure in order to see the body of Christ reach the world. People who have the genuine gift of giving are overjoyed that they can give time, that they can use their talents, and that they can give of the treasure God entrusts to them. Let me tell you two quick examples. My brother Gene has the gift of giving. He's a behind-the-scenes, let-me-at-it, let-me-do-this kind of man. He also has the gift of faith, so he is always dreaming bigger than most of us are able to. He is a visionary who is willing to give time, talent, and treasure to see that future happen.

R. G. LeTourneau is another example. For years he wanted to be a pastor. He believed God had called him to be a missionary or a minister. But the more he pursued it, the more it became clear he was *not* supposed to be in vocational ministry. Instead, God gave him the ability to be an engineer of earth-moving equipment (Caterpillar tractors), and he became very wealthy. So, LeTourneau made the kingdom decision to "reverse tithe"—to live on 10 percent of his income and give away 90 percent. He never became the preacher he wanted to be. But God combined his gift of giving with some amazing engineering skills to produce substantive resources for the kingdom of God to be funded for effective ministry.

The gift of *mercy* is the capacity to care, to come alongside, to empathize, and to be Jesus-with-skin-on to those in need. People with this gift want to bring relief to immediate needs. They feel compassion toward those in the hospital and those struggling with physical, financial, emotional, or spiritual situations. People with the gift of mercy have deep empathy that makes them effective in relating God's love to those who are hurting.

The gift of *hospitality* is the ability to communicate a warm welcome that enriches people and makes them feel comfortable in unfamiliar surroundings. People with this gift create environments where others feel valued and cared for, especially regarding food, lodging, and fellowship. Hospitable people make friends easily and seek ways to connect with others in meaningful relationships.

### Ministry Protection Gifts

Ministry protection gifts are those that challenge and guard the flock. These gifts keep the body of Christ a safe place where people can grow. If a local body of believers lacks the gifts of knowledge, wisdom, faith, and discernment, then evil, untruth, and deception can get in and wreak havoc.

The gifts of knowledge and wisdom are companion gifts. Believers with the gift of *knowledge* have exceptional insight into the truths of God's Word. They put effort into learning as much as possible about Scripture, systematizing and summarizing it in order to explain it to others. The gift of *wisdom* is the ability to use God's Word to transform daily life into spiritual service. People with this gift can sort through conflict and confusion and offer direction for making godly decisions. They have the insight to understand how knowledge can best be applied to specific situations.

The gift of *faith* is the ability to see God's invisible plan and believe it, despite the current visible reality. It takes no faith to believe that the snowball rolling downhill will keep going. But it takes faith to believe that the snowball you're currently pushing uphill will finally make it over the hilltop. Those with the gift of faith have an unwavering confidence in God's power to bring unity out of hostility, peace out of storms, and good out of evil.

The gift of *discernment* is the ability to determine whether something or someone is of God, of the flesh (the human nature), or of the adversary, the Evil One. It is the ability to distinguish truth from error and sincerity from hypocrisy. Those with discernment are able to sense the presence of evil. Did you know the Bible teaches that Satan masquerades as an angel of light (2 Corinthians 11:14)? In this way, he is able to twist things and confuse issues. People with the gift of discernment can listen to something and know whether it is from God or not.

## Ministry Sign Gifts

The last category of gifts is ministry sign gifts. These are often used as God's vehicle to extend the work of God into an unreached area. They concern evangelism and obedience—and these gifts are very controversial. If you're a new Christian or not yet a Christian, these may be some of the gifts that have made you feel uncomfortable. You may have seen people dancing, shouting, or rolling in the aisles. Let me say that I believe God still employs these gifts today. But I also believe they are often abused and distorted, whereas God calls for decency and order in his church.

If what I've just said troubles you in any way, please read 1 Corinthians 14 for more insight on this issue. The church of Corinth had severe spiritual problems. They had all the gifts we've mentioned, but they abused their gifts by having a "magic party" every weekend. The church meeting was chaotic, and nobody was being drawn closer to God. They promoted people who had "showy" gifts, instead of promoting unity and love. In 1 Corinthians 14, Paul corrected this behavior.

Four gifts make up the ministry sign gifts: healing, miracles, tongues, and interpretation of tongues. The first is the gift of *healing:* the supernatural intervention to produce physical, spiritual, and emotional restoration. People with this gift have a divine enablement to bring healing to others through prayer, touch, or speaking words. I have personally been part of prayer experiences in which God brought healing to a person through touch. I've also been part of prayer experiences after which sick people worsened and died. In some cases God brings healing through gifted individuals; in other cases, he does not. *Remember, though, if you get distracted and focus on the gift and not the giver, you will get catawampus to the world.*

The gift of *miracles* is supernatural intervention in the spiritual or natural realm. People with this gift can perform acts of supernatural power in order to authenticate the gospel and give glory to God. Let me give you two examples from the Bible. The fifth chapter of Mark tells us that a man possessed by many demons came to Jesus. The man was so strong that no chains could bind him. Jesus drove the demons out of him, and from that point forward, this man was clothed and in his right mind and began testifying about Jesus in his hometown. An example in the Old Testament occurred in the life of Joshua. During a battle with the Amorites, Joshua prayed to God for the sun to stand still so that the Israelites could finish winning their battle against their enemy. "Joshua said to the LORD in the presence of Israel: 'Sun, stand still over Gibeon, and you, moon, over the Valley of Aijalon.' So the sun stood still, and the moon stopped, till the nation avenged itself on its enemies" (Joshua 10:12–13). That was a miracle of God done through the agency of one of his children.

Does God do miracles every day through his children? You bet! I wouldn't ever want to say, "That gift is gone. God doesn't do those kinds of miracles anymore." God can do whatever God wants to do! And I will continue to pray for miracles. If events don't happen the way I want them to, I will leave the results to God, because he is in charge, I'm not.

The next gift is *tongues*. There are two aspects to the gift of tongues. I find Scripture to be fairly clear about these two aspects, but reasonable Christians often disagree on these two points. The gift of tongues is both a personal prayer language that helps build a believer's spirit as well as a supernatural ability to speak an unlearned language for the purpose of evangelism. I have letters in my files from missionaries who had been in situations on a foreign field where they had not yet learned the language of the people they were supposed to reach, but God immediately granted them the ability to speak that language so people would come to know Christ—and they did! God is still using that gift for kingdom purposes.

People have different beliefs about public expressions of the gift of tongues and interpretation of tongues (interpreting a personal prayer language publicly for the sake of edifying the whole body). In 1 Corinthians 14, Paul said not to do anything in a public assembly that would cause an unbeliever to "freak out." Now, that's a very loose translation, but that is the gist of it. Don't do anything in a public assembly that might cause an unbeliever to say, "These people are crazy! What are they doing?" Because of this, we make worship services at our church very understandable, very accessible, and very easy for nonbelievers to connect with, for the sake of the good news of Jesus Christ.

God gave all these gifts to the church so that we could serve him effectively. God gave you a gift, and his gift is a treasure, ready to be unwrapped. He wants you to use it for his glory and honor. If you don't know what your gift is, then find out. If you know what it is but haven't been using it, then use it. If you have been using it, then keep developing it.

One day, Pastor Alan Redpath went to call on a woman who had been crippled for nine years. Before he entered the room to see her, he tried to prepare himself. *What am I going to say to this woman? How can I bring God's encouragement to somebody who has been disabled for nine years?* As he walked into the room and began to speak to her, she interrupted him and said, "You know, Pastor, I wouldn't give up these last nine years for anything. After being confined in this hospital bed, I began to wonder what in the world God wanted me to do, and I felt that God called me to intercede in prayer. So, I've been making a list of missionaries and pastors and evangelists and Christian leaders, and I've taken it as my personal place in the plan of God to pray for those people and to see what God will do."

Redpath wrote the following about his encounter with the woman:

> Eternity alone will reveal how much I owe as a minister of the Gospel to the prayers of that dear woman, who, for so long, labored in obscurity in the service of the King of kings, Lord of lords. Let therefore be neither strife nor envy nor contempt nor ill will between those who are the valiant men holding key positions and those who are doing the unseen, unrecognized, unreported tasks. Both are needful, both are useful, both are dependent upon each other and neither can be spared. (Alan Redpath, *Victorious Christian Service: Studies in the Book of Nehemiah* [Santa Ana, CA: Calvary Chapel Publishing, 2005], 157)

Discover your gift—so that God receives the glory!

## LANDMARK 14:
# An Invitation

Your spiritual gifts are a treasure. Embarking on the quest to discover your gifts can pull you into the adventure of a lifetime—or rather—of an eternity.

*The kingdom of heaven is like treasure hidden in a field. When a man found it, he hid it again, and then in his joy went and sold all he had and bought that field. (Matthew 13:44)*

It was a dark and stormy night. Charcoal clouds hurried across the sky, dropping wave upon wave of pelting rain. Wind howled down the mountainside and through the valley, sending tree branches into a frenzied dance. The only light came from sporadic bursts of lightning that crackled through the air and stood Donna's hair on end.

With her power out, Donna huddled under an afghan on the couch, reading a novel by candlelight. She was partway through chapter five when there came a sudden pounding at the back door. Instantly, Donna was on her feet, heart thumping, and all senses on alert.

There it was again, an insistent pounding that Donna felt compelled to answer. She picked up the candle, walked through the house, and slowly opened the back door. A mysterious stranger stood there, the torrential rain pouring over the brim of his hat like a waterfall, keeping her from getting a good look at his face. He never spoke, he just handed Donna an aged leather box; and then he melted back into the storm.

Donna's fingers tingled as they touched the box. Gingerly, she carried it to the kitchen table and set it down. After lighting a few more candles, Donna sat down and opened the box. Inside was a rolled up, weathered parchment, its edges worn away. Trembling, Donna unrolled the parchment and gasped.

It was a map. A treasure map. And it appeared to be authentic.

> Donna studied the map late into the night. Then, she gathered a few supplies and stuffed them into a knapsack. She rolled up the map and gently slid it into a leather pouch that she had hung around her neck. Donna glanced around her living room, her eyes landing on a stack of mail on the coffee table, on a box of files she had brought home from work, on the half-read novel and crumpled afghan lying on the floor where she had dropped them.
>
> Then, map thumping softly against her heart, Donna walked out the door of her house and locked it behind her. She bent her head against the wind and strode into the storm, in search of buried treasure.

A treasure map. Buried treasure. What images they evoke: the search, the mystery, the adventure. Pirates, battles, and swordfights. Sworn allegiances, bitter enemies. Rough voyages, costly detours. Blood, sweat, tears. Passion, zeal, excitement. Plenty of frantic moments; never a dull one. Great sacrifice and untold rewards.

Gets your heart pumping, doesn't it? But what does any of that have to do with spiritual gifts?

*Everything!* If the thought of discovering the spiritual gifts God has given you doesn't get your heart pumping with the same level of excitement as the story you've just read, then something is horribly wrong. The church has done you a terrible disservice.

Hear this: when describing our spiritual journey, God never used the tame sort of imagery we often use when we "churchify" our faith. Read your Bible again, this time with new eyes. Spiritual life is not a stroll; it's an adventure with high stakes, a struggle against a powerful enemy, a battle that requires armor and the ability to stand firm (Ephesians 6).

The kingdom of God is not a nice addition to your already full life. "The kingdom of heaven is like treasure hidden in a field. When a man found it, he hid it again, and then in his joy went and sold all he had and bought that field" (Matthew 13:44). See how often God raises the call to his people to seek, to search, to explore the depths of life and of living for him. See the promise that we serve a God who "rewards those who earnestly seek him" (Hebrews 11:6).

As you contemplate finding your place in life and ministry, keep in mind that God has given you a map that leads to an amazing treasure. The map is faithful; so is the mapmaker. The one who buried the treasure wants nothing more than for you to find it.

We will be looking in this chapter at what that treasure is, what the treasure map looks like, and how to follow the map to the riches God has for you.

But before we start, hear the echoes of adventurers before us who also followed the map: "We are hard pressed on every side, but not crushed; perplexed, but not in despair; persecuted, but not abandoned; struck down, but not destroyed" (2 Corinthians 4:8–9).

Listen as they pray for others to see the treasure they found: "I pray that the eyes of your heart may be enlightened in order that you may know the hope to which he has called you, the riches of his glorious inheritance in his holy people, and his incomparably great power for us who believe" (Ephesians 1:18–19).

Hear Jesus call us to the hunt:

> So I say to you: Ask and it will be given to you; seek and you will find; knock and the door will be opened to you. For everyone who asks receives; the one who seeks finds; and to the one who knocks, the door will be opened.
>
> Which of you fathers, if your son asks for a fish, will give him a snake instead? Or if he asks for an egg, will give him a scorpion? If you then, though you are evil, know how to give good gifts to your children, how much more will your Father in heaven give the Holy Spirit to those who ask him! (Luke 11:9–13)

Is your heart pounding yet? I hope so. God is calling you to an adventure. Dare to grab hold of the map and head out into the storm. Dare to leave your half-read novel and enter into the real-life story God has for you.

---

LANDMARK 15:

# Begin the Treasure Hunt

Now and then, people stumble across a treasure by accident. But most seekers of treasure have to do just that—seek. When they are ready to take that first step toward the treasure, it helps to know in what direction to be heading—and what some of the landmarks are along the way.

You may be ready to start looking for your gift mix and to discover how God has wired you to make a difference. As you do so, know that God takes every believer on a personalized journey in this regard; your route to the treasure will look different from mine. There are, however, certain landmarks that show up on everyone's quest. So, if you're looking for a place to start or feeling a bit lost on your journey, try heading toward one of the landmarks discussed below.

## Prayer

Remember, God doesn't want you to be ignorant about your gifts (1 Corinthians 12:1). And, he promises to give wisdom to you when you ask for it (James 1:5). Consider employing a prayer project in which every day for thirty days you ask God to reveal your gifts to you. Remember that spiritual gifts are different from your innate or inborn skills. They are grace gifts that God's Spirit gives to each believer in Christ. Pray that the Holy Spirit will guide your ability to distinguish what you are good at from the ways he has specifically gifted you for ministry.

## Community

Spiritual growth happens in community with other Christians—not in "meetings," but in experiences of true biblical community where the "one anothers" of the New Testament are practiced and shared. In biblical community, your gifts and abilities will be recognized and affirmed by those Christians with whom you spend time. You may even want to ask believers who know you well what gifts they see in you. (You can then confirm or discard their observations through prayer and experience in ministry.)

## The Bible

The apostle Paul gave us four lists of spiritual gifts in the New Testament. Though the lists are probably not exhaustive, they are a great place to start. Spend some time reading in Romans 12, 1 Corinthians 12, Ephesians 4, and 1 Peter 4. Which gifts seem to jump out at you as gifts you think you may possess? To gain further insight, consider studying Bible passages about people who exhibited the gifts you think God may have given you.

## A Test

If the very idea of taking a test makes you sweat and nibble nervously on your pencil, take a deep breath. A spiritual gifts inventory is not a pass/fail endeavor. Nor is it the final say on your gifts. Rather, it's a series of questions that can help shape your thinking about the ways God has gifted you for ministry. In the appendix of this book, we've provided a list of online spiritual gifts assessments, recommended for you to use as one step in the process of confirming what your gifts may be.

## Experience

Because spiritual gifts are given to have an impact on the church and the world, at some point you will need to take action and gain some experience in ministry. If you're unsure what your gifts might be, participate in a broad range of activities that would tap into different gifts. Teach a class. Give sacrificially. Share your faith.

Watch to see what God does, how people respond, and what you think and feel. When you serve in an area of gifting, you will experience a comfort level and fruitfulness that others—doing the same thing without those same gifts—will not fully experience. If you have some idea what your gifts may be, dive into activities where those gifts would likely be helpful. Watch how God uses your experience to refine your understanding of the gifts he has provided you.

In the adventure of finding your spiritual gifts, the landmarks we've just talked about can keep you going in the right direction. Spend some time praying today about what landmark God may want you to visit—or revisit—next.

---

LANDMARK 16:

# Finding Gifts in Community

Ever try to put together a softball team from scratch? A group of interested players shows up for the first practice. They throw the ball around, not knowing where they fit, not knowing how they will play together. A few weeks later and several games into the season, the same group of players has become a team. The ball speeds around the diamond, every throw hitting its mark; the players anticipate each other's moves; confidence and camaraderie infuse the dugout.

How does that happen? How does a ragtag group of people with ball gloves become a softball team? It probably looks something like this: they start with a series of practices. They throw the ball around. They practice batting, and they rotate players to different positions. While having a good time, laughing, enjoying the exercise, they are also sizing up each player's strengths and weaknesses.

After a few practices, they have a good idea where to position each player for the first game. Ideally, positioning should not become a competition for choice positions, but a gradual recognition of each player's strongest area of contribution. After a few games, the team has shifted the lineup a couple of times and perhaps moved players around on the field. The players have learned where they perform best. Not that everything is finalized—changes may still need to be made at some point. But for now, the team is solid. The players know their positions and their contributions to the team.

If you were interviewing players, you might hear comments such as these:

- "Dave's got such a good arm. We knew that if we could get the batter to ground to short, then we could pull off a double play."
- "Sheila might not be the strongest fielder, but because she is so consistent at the plate, I would hate to see her out of the lineup."
- "I can't run worth beans. But I knew that if I could draw the walk, then we could put Chris in to run for me—and he would get himself into scoring position, and we would have a chance to tie the game."

Did you hear it? The awareness of one's own contribution as well as that of each teammate. The humility and grace to give room for a teammate's strength to compensate for your weakness. The delight of working toward a common goal and seeing each member of the team play an important part in achieving that goal.

How does that happen? How does an unorganized group of people with ball gloves become a softball team?

And how does an unorganized group of believers with gifts and abilities, strengths and weaknesses, varied personalities and experiences become a biblically functioning church?

It probably looks something like this: they start with a series of practices. Call them what you will: home groups, Bible studies, ministry teams, potlucks. They throw their ideas around. They try some ministry activities, and they rotate people to different positions. They are having a good time, laughing, enjoying the activity and the company, but in the process, they are also sizing up each other's strengths and weaknesses. It might not be a conscious thing, but it happens.

After a while, the believers have a good idea where to position themselves for ministry. In an ideal scenario, this is not a competition for choice positions, but a gradual recognition of each believer's strongest area of contribution. Not that everything is finalized—changes may still need to be made at some point. But for now, the community is solid. People know their positions and their contributions to the team.

If you were interviewing them, you might hear comments such as these:

- "Abby's such a compassionate listener. I knew that if I could introduce her to Shawna, Abby could really be a big help to her right now."
- "Ed might not like to talk in front of people, but because he's so great at making people feel welcome in our class, I would hate to lose him."
- "I might not be a gifted evangelist, but I know that if I invite my neighbor to our home group, then Sheri will explain the faith clearly in her teaching."

Did you hear it? The awareness of one's own contribution as well as that of other believers. The humility and grace to give room for a fellow believer's strength to compensate for your weakness. The delight of working toward a common goal—and seeing each member of the community play an important part in achieving that goal.

So, if you're a bit unsure about your gifts—about your contribution to the team—maybe you need to show up at practice. Throw the ball around a bit. Take some batting practice, and let your teammates help you hone your skills and find your position on the team. And you can do the same for them.

---

LANDMARK 17:

# Don't Be in Such a Hurry!

*Whoever is patient has great understanding, but one who is quick-tempered displays folly. (Proverbs 14:29)*

Moses is *the man.* He had a huge job to do, and he did it well—with God's power. Among Christians and Jews, he is revered as an uberleader who led the Israelites out of Egyptian slavery, and many Christians view him as a type of Christ.

One day, however, Moses made a bad choice, and it cost him dearly. It was an issue of patience and trust.

The Israelites were grumbling again, frustrated with Moses and quarreling with him about their lack of water (Numbers 20). Moses went before God, facedown, and got his answer: "Speak to that rock . . . and it will pour out its water."

But Moses, grieving his sister's recent death and frustrated with the rebellion of God's people, stood and shouted at the people, "Listen, you rebels!" What an introduction to a speech! If things hadn't turned out so badly, we might admire it. But instead of speaking to the rock as God had commanded, Moses struck the rock twice with his staff. Moses paid a price for his direct and public disobedience: he never set foot in the Promised Land. A high price indeed.

Losing our patience costs us dearly as well, each time we do it. We yell and break our child's heart, one piece at a time. We swerve our car in anger and risk the lives of our family members and of others on the road. We speak our mind harshly and lose a friendship forever.

Anger isn't the only area where patience is required of us. Finding a spouse may take years. Finding a good job may be an extended process. Finding the right house may require a long search—and more than one offer. Finding a parking space may not happen on your first loop through the parking lot. The need for patience is a thread woven consistently through our lives.

Yet, sometimes we expect to discover our place in ministry immediately, bypassing the perseverance and patience required in every other facet of our lives. Finding *your place* is a wonderful and worthwhile pursuit—but it may be just that: a pursuit. You may have to search for the right opportunity and niche for weeks or months before something finally clicks. Keep the following truths in mind as you embark on the journey: (1) finding your niche in ministry might take some time, and (2) finding your niche in ministry, like anything truly important, is worth waiting for. So, don't give up if you don't find it right away!

Make it your goal to *not* short circuit the process God wants to take you through in finding your place. I would hate for you to "pull a Moses" and miss out on the Promised Land God has for you!

---

## LANDMARK 18:
# Wild and Holy Song

I walk through empty halls of life,
longing for a springtime breeze;
shuffle through my everydays,

wishing somehow I were free.
Then I hear Your voice gain entrance
to my hungry heart and mind,
and You call me to come follow
and see what I will find.
Your voice carries deepest music
when You sing to me my name;
I know there's nothing here to lose
and everything to gain.
So I'll lock the door behind me,
leave my tame and lukewarm faith;
run to the wild and untamed land,
wind of Your Spirit in my face.

There's a life here for the living.
There's a treasure to be found.
There's a joy for those who by God's power
turn earth to holy ground.
There's an adventure to be taken.
There's a vision to be seen.
There's a path for you when by God's grace
your spirit dares to dream.
There's an enemy to be conquered.
There's a captive who's been wronged.
There's a mission for those who by God's love
hear His wild and holy song.

Now I run through barren wastelands,
leap over rocky streams.
By day I'm fueled by burning fire,
by night I'm fueled by dreams.
I've fought the fiercest battles.

I've made the truest friends.
I've wept hot tears of sorrow,
and I've laughed from deep within.
I've found the place You have for me.
I've found where I belong—
where You teach my hands, my heart
to dance to the rhythm of Your song.

There is no ordinary,
there is no commonplace—
when in each task I hear your music,
in each child I see Your face.
There's a life here for the living.
There's a treasure to be found.
There's a joy for those
who by God's power turn earth to holy ground.
There's an adventure to be taken.
There's a vision to be seen.
There's a path for you
when by God's grace your spirit dares to dream.
There's an enemy to be conquered.
There's a captive who's been wronged.
There's a mission for those
who by God's love hear His wild and holy song.
Hear the Spirit singing
His wild and holy song,
through time and all creation
to the timid and the strong.
Sing over me,
Holy Spirit.
Sing over me
Your wild and holy song.

## LANDMARK 19:
# The eBay Mentality

Imagine seeing this on the nightly news: someone sneaks into a department store during the night and switches all the price tags. Plasma screen televisions are now $4.99, while a candy bar will cost you $25.00. Chaos ensues.

But, really, don't we live in a society where the price tags are constantly morphing? Items no longer have an inherent value. Their value is determined by how much they will fetch on eBay on any given day. If many people are looking to collect Pez candy dispensers this year, then suddenly your childhood leftovers may be worth a small fortune. If a trend in Southwest decor begins to fade, then chances are you will be stuck with that bronze coyote sculpture you shelled out the big bucks for a few years back.

Sounds right, doesn't it? That's the way capitalism works. It's the American way. Supply and demand.

But what happens when we carry this way of thinking into the church? Well, if you're in a community that values fellowship more than reaching out, and you have the gift of evangelism, then you're out of luck—a second-class citizen. But if you're a teacher or a person with the gift of shepherding or encouragement, you will fit right in. In a community that focuses its attention on the sign gifts (tongues, miracles), your perceived value will rise or fall based on whether you possess those particular gifts.

All of a sudden, we have developed a Christian caste system based on spiritual gifts. Those with the "right" gifts are accorded first-class status, and the rest of us will be flying coach. Feelings of superiority or inferiority crop up. Cliques develop. Resentment flares. Division runs rampant. And we start earnestly petitioning God for the gifts that will move us up the church ladder, as though God were likely to put the trendier gifts up for auction on eBay.

Doesn't sound right anymore, does it? And here's why: unlike the cacophony of collectibles you will find in an online auction, spiritual gifts do not derive their value from the people who admire or desire them. They derive their value from the God who created them and gives them to his children to mature each other.

God tells us that every single gift is important and vital to the community of believers. No one gift is more or less important than another. So then, every single believer is important and vital to the community of believers, with no one person being more or less important than another (1 Corinthians 12:4–31).

There's a passage in Matthew where Jesus told a parable about what it will be like when he returns and people come before him to be judged. In the parable, the king (Jesus) says to the people, "Truly I tell you, whatever you did for one of the least of these brothers and sisters of mine, you did for me" (Matthew 25:40). In other words, in every encounter we have with another believer—and potentially in every encounter we have with an unbeliever—we encounter Jesus. The person with the gift of helps is just as likely to encounter Jesus as is the person with the gift of prophecy. The person working in a church classroom full of two-year-olds is just as likely to meet the Savior as is the person greeting people at the door or the person singing on the stage. How do we dare say that one encounter with Jesus—one opportunity to serve our Master—is more important or less important than another? We dare not.

Don't be fooled by an eBay mentality.

# Jesus with Skin On

"God loves you."

We've heard and read that phrase countless times. We may even know the Bible verses that prove it. God demonstrated his love for us like this: "While we were still sinners, Christ died for us" (Romans 5:8). "For God so loved the world that he gave his one and only Son, that whoever believes in him shall not perish but have eternal life" (John 3:16).

God loves us so much that he gave us Jesus. And that would be enough, don't you think? I mean, eternal life is hardly a gift to scoff at. But God didn't stop there. God loves us so much that he gave us each other. He gave us fellow believers. He gave us the church.

Sometimes we say that we need to watch the way we act toward non-Christians, because we might be "the only Jesus-with-skin-on they ever meet." And that is true. But I need Jesus-with-skin-on as much as anyone else does. Don't you?

People are not likely to spot the first-century Galilean Jesus walking down the street today. But they might see you. And if Jesus is living in you through the Holy Spirit, he could use your hands to help carry their loads. He could use your smile to refresh their hearts. He could use your resources to meet their needs. He could love them through you, because

- every time a believer shows love to another, that person is receiving God's love;
- every time a Christian cheers someone through the gift of encouragement, God himself is cheering that someone;
- every time a follower of Christ speaks truth to a friend in the power of the Holy Spirit, God is speaking truth to that friend;

- every time a disciple of Jesus comforts a fellow human being with words of mercy, God is comforting that human's soul.

When Jesus walked the Galilean countryside, he healed the sick, he taught with power, he drew people to the Father. He confronted sin, encouraged the oppressed, and led a devoted core of disciples. But he couldn't reach everyone. He was God, yes; but he was for that season confined to a human form, to time, and to geography.

But what if, when Jesus went back to the Father in heaven, he didn't leave his followers alone but sent his Holy Spirit to them, to live inside of them? And what if the Holy Spirit gave gifts to all the believers, so they could do in their own times and geographies all the things Jesus had done in his (Ephesians 4:7–13)?

God loved us so much that he gave us Jesus. What if he loves us so much still that he gives us each other to be Jesus-with-skin-on, exponentially?

---( 4 )---

# YOU FIT IN THE FAMILY

Spiritual growth happens in community. I'm not saying you can't have a spiritual experience alone. On the contrary, I actually urge people as they are growing spiritually to find moments of solitude—moments when they can literally (as said in Psalm 46) "be still, and know that I am God." However, relationships are also very important aspects of God's plan for our lives. God places his children in communities of faith where we can be supported and safeguarded as we discover our gifts.

## A Loving Place to Grow Up

God's plan for your life requires that you be in loving relationships with others. In John 13:34–35, we see Jesus at the end of his earthly ministry. Knowing his time was short, knowing he would soon leave this earth, Jesus spoke these important words: "A new command I give you." When some people get to the end of their earthly time, they try to set things in order. They make sure everything is taken care of, that their family will be well attended to, and that their last wishes and instructions are known. That is what Jesus was doing. "A new command I give you: Love one another. As I have loved you, so you must love one another. By this everyone will know that you are my disciples, if you love one another."

Jesus commanded us to be in loving relationships with one another. He commanded us to have a circle of people with whom we can meaningfully relate. In our church, we designed our weekend services to enable people to come and enjoy the "anonymity." This was a purposeful choice. When you come into our church, you don't have to tell anyone your life story, and you don't have to be vulnerable or transparent with anybody. You can just come and check it out. You can do that for weeks or months. Sometimes people do it for years.

Though we invite people into the tent of anonymity, we do so knowing it's not the place of ultimate spiritual health. We explain clearly that to get to spiritual health, you must move from the tent of anonymity down the road into community, where you can be in solid relationships with others.

Many times, men in our culture are taught early in life to be self-reliant and independent. It's considered the pinnacle of success to be able to say, "I'm a self-made man." I suggest, however, that everyone stands on the shoulders of those who have gone before us. I don't know all that you've been through, but the freedom you have today to declare yourself a self-made man or a self-made woman is possible because you live in a land where people before you paid with their blood the price of freedom. So, at the very minimum, I would say that even if your circumstances are such that you have accomplished a lot because of your efforts, remember that others made it possible for you to pursue the freedom to be who you are. All of us stand on the shoulders of someone else. All of us have people who have invested in our lives, even if that investment was in the systems or governments that shape the culture in which we live. If you are a follower of Christ or you're searching for God, then please remember that you stand on the shoulders of others who have gone before you.

A critical aspect to being in loving relationships with others involves knowing this: *you were made "special-order."* That's a powerful fact to understand. Some people think that God has a widget factory in heaven that makes people in only four or five basic varieties. However, the Bible teaches that you are a unique human being. No one else on the planet is like you. Let's look again at a well-known Bible passage, which we introduced in Landmark 2: Psalm 139:13–16.

> For you created my inmost being;
> you knit me together in my mother's womb.
> I praise you because I am fearfully and wonderfully
>     made;
> your works are wonderful,
> I know that full well.
> My frame was not hidden from you
> when I was made in the secret place,
> when I was woven together in the depths of the earth.
> Your eyes saw my unformed body;
> all the days ordained for me were written in your
>     book
> before one of them came to be.

As parents and grandparents, our task is to identify and call forth—to understand and to draw out—the uniqueness God created in each of our children. Each child has distinctive characteristics that parents can develop. Sometimes, even by age four or five, some children begin demonstrating the traits of an attorney; they have the ability to brilliantly argue their case. Others reveal a teaching gene and instruct their parents on how things should be. Other children have an engineering gene and start taking things apart because they're fascinated by how things work. We are unique creations of God and precious in his sight.

## Healthy Cautions for a Loving Family

Just as God puts children in families, so God also puts believers in church families that provide home groups, ministries, classes, and a variety of other ways for people to connect in loving relationships. That does not mean you should be "best friends" with fifty people, or even fifteen. There should be a few people who know and love you well enough to speak life and hope to you as well as to challenge you when you're doing less than your best. In light of our need for close, trusted friends, there are some cautions I'd like to share with you.

### Caution: *Projection*

The first caution is the temptation of *projection:* when others tell you what they see in you because it's really what they see in themselves. This happened to me in my early twenties. It was a very stressful period of my life as I settled into ministry and continued my education. I would often ask God and myself, *Where is my future?* One day, I asked a close friend to sit down with me in a restaurant, and I told him of my struggle. I asked him, "Where do you see me in five years?" His answer startled me: "I see you as a missionary to China."

Well, of course, there's nothing wrong with being a missionary to China. It is a wonderful call of God. But his answer was a reflection of *his* personal struggle, not mine. He had been feeling God call him to international missions. His answer wasn't really from God to him for me; it was from God to him *for him.* And that is where it should have stayed.

Isaiah 6 contains a great passage. When Isaiah was in the temple of God, he saw a vision and heard the voice of God saying, "Whom shall I send? And who will go for us?" Did Isaiah respond to God saying, "Here I am Lord, *send him*"? No, of course not. He actually said, "Here am I. Send me!" When you invite people into your life, be discerning about what they say to you. We're all guilty of projection from time to time.

## Caution: *Elevation*

A second caution relates to the issue of *elevation*. Elevation occurs when others puff you up because of your gifting. That is, people overemphasize the effects of your gifts. They may even start to believe that you are so gifted by God you don't have ordinary struggles. While it is helpful to have people speak life and affirmation into your service for God, you must be cautious not to forget that everything you are and everything you have, you received by grace, not by merit. Gifts are not things to boast about. Be careful of elevating yourself or letting others do it for you.

## Caution: *Rejection*

The third caution is the flipside to elevation, *rejection*. Rejection takes place when people see *no good* in you. Every time they speak to you, they speak toxins to your soul. They stick pinpricks in the balloons of your life. These are negative, critical people, and we must recognize them as such and not allow them access to the interior parts of our souls! Just as the people who elevate can cause you to think wrongly (by believing you're uncommonly good), so people who reject you can also cause you to think wrongly (by believing you are a failure). Another way to say this is *hurt people hurt people*. People who are themselves hurting tend to wound others as a way of life. Be careful who you allow to have access to your soul, and eliminate the elevation and rejection.

God has a unique design for your life and wants your relationships with others to be characterized by love—the kind of love described in 1 Corinthians 13:1–8:

> If I speak in the tongues of men and of angels, but do not have love, I am only a resounding gong or a clanging cymbal. If I have the gift of prophecy and can fathom all mysteries and all knowledge, and if I have a faith that can move mountains, but do not have love, I am nothing. If I give all I possess to the poor and give over my body to hardship that I may boast, but do not have love, I gain nothing.
>
> Love is patient, love is kind. It does not envy, it does not boast, it is not proud. It does not dishonor others, it is not self-seeking, it is not easily angered, it keeps no record of wrongs. Love does not delight in evil but rejoices with the truth. It always protects, always trusts, always hopes, always perseveres.
>
> Love never fails.

What a powerful description of the nature of loving relationships that God calls us to! This standard for love is high; the reality we experience is often low. But this passage is not about natural human love. It's not about your love as a husband or wife, mother or father, grandma or grandpa, aunt or uncle, or friend. This passage is about the nature of God's love. To the extent that you allow God's love to flow through you to other people, you will be able to experience a 1 Corinthians 13 kind of love in your life and in the ministry of your gifts.

## What S.H.A.P.E. Are You?

I believe that we are best served when we have a realistic assessment of ourselves, coupled with the loving input of those we are in relationship with. Often it is helpful to have a template or grid through which we can assess our various strengths and weaknesses. I've used one particular tool that I would commend to you. At Saddleback Community Church in Mission Viejo, California, Pastor Rick Warren and his team promote a concept called S.H.A.P.E. Each letter in this acronym stands for an important truth about finding your niche in God's plan. These truths may help you remember that God has designed you and shaped you uniquely for ministry.

**S**—stands for *spiritual gifts.* Spiritual gifts are a unique tool that God gives you to grow and develop the body of Christ. Your gifts benefit and serve others.

**H**—stands for your *heart,* what you are passionate about. If when finished with a task you feel dead tired but deeply fulfilled, then you are probably operating within the realm of your passion. Sadly, many times people say to me, "I used to be passionate about music lessons (or painting, or you fill in the blank), but then I got sidetracked." They may have stopped for any number of reasons—a financial barrier, a lack of time, or a sudden tragedy. Know this: no matter how far you have moved away from your passion, keep coming back to it!

**A**—stands for *ability.* Abilities are the natural talents and skills you possess, not to be confused with *spiritual gifts.* One day a member of our church was approached by a friend in his small group. "I think your spiritual gift is carpentry," his friend told him. After looking through a list of biblical spiritual gifts, but not finding carpentry among them, he told me, "The spiritual gift I believe I have is mercy. Carpentry is a skill I'm good at." I asked if he ever used his woodworking skills to encourage or help others through a difficult time. "Oh, yes," he answered, "all the time." So, his spiritual gift is mercy; his passion to help people often combines with his skills in woodworking. They fit together.

**P**—stands for *personality*. We all have one. Some of us are extroverts; some are introverts. Some of us are task oriented; some are relationship oriented. We are simply wired in different ways. God designed your unique personality as a piece of the overall picture of your service to him in ministry.

**E**—stands for *experience*. God never wastes a wound; he never wastes an experience. I read an article about Stormie Omartian, author of *The Power of a Praying Wife*. She experienced horrible abuse as a child. Today, when she speaks in different settings, Stormie gives testimony that although God didn't cause the abuse to happen, he has used those early experiences as a point of ministry later in her life. God has the power to take whatever experiences happen in our lives and use them for his glory, for the benefit of others, and for our maturity. (For more information, visit www.shapediscovery.com).

## Your Five-Hundred-Year Investment Plan

God's plan for your life is described as the straight and narrow. But maybe you've taken some detours. If so, ask him, "God, will you restore the issues of my life and bring me to where you want me to be?" He will take you—wherever you are on the detour of life—and move you forward to fulfill his dream for you. God never *causes* those detours. It grieves his heart when we take them; but if we turn toward him, he will use the pain and the wound to equip us to serve him.

Friends, we are in a battle, a literal war; we have a spiritual adversary. In John 10:10, Jesus said, "The thief comes only to steal and kill and destroy; I have come that they may have life, and have it to the full." God's plan for your life involves other people. But Satan, the adversary of your soul, does not want you to be in relationship with other people—he wants you to be disconnected from people, feeling isolated and lonely rather than feeling special. You may face many battles where Satan gets a foothold in your soul through your negative feelings. Satan can then lead you on a detour away from the right path. You may lose the battle, but you *will* win the war because you are on the *winning side.*

If you are a follower of Jesus Christ—if you are in right relationship with God—or if you're wondering where God fits in your life, please understand that God has a place for you in his plan. He has a purpose for your life and has given you spiritual gifts to fulfill that purpose. As you pursue that purpose, you will develop relationships with others, and the unique, distinctive, custom-made things about you will come to the surface, enabling you to find your place on God's winning team.

You might think that an adventure of this kind is simply a way of getting more workers for a church's ministries. The reality is that God is inviting us to the adventure of a lifetime. He wants our lives to be invested in those things that will stand for time and eternity. I recently heard a teacher ask, "What is the five-hundred-year plan for your life?" The more I thought about it, the more I began to feel convicted about that whole concept.

God did not place you on this earth to merely live for sixty, seventy, eighty years. He placed you on this earth to invest in his kingdom work, both for now and for eternity. If Jesus doesn't come back for five hundred more years, what is your long-term investment plan? Ask yourself, *What am I doing today to invest in the lives of others, and to make God's kingdom purposes come to pass, so that God's work is lived out in our world long after I'm dead?*

We watch *Animal Planet* at our house from time to time, and often we see episodes about lions hunting in the wild. When lions are chasing a herd of wildebeests, the herd is never in trouble when it stays together. Can you guess when animals get into trouble? It is when the weak, the wounded, or the young get isolated from the herd.

The Bible says that we have an adversary of our soul. He prowls about like a roaring lion seeking someone to devour. When you are where God wants you to be, when you are in that place where you are custom-made and designed to be, you are not at risk. If you fly solo, you are at risk. God invites you to the adventure of a lifetime, an adventure intended to be shared in community. Join with others, and walk alongside them as you discover your place in God's plan!

---

## LANDMARK 21:
# The Love Factor

Spiritual growth happens within relationships. Discovering your gifts within a community of faith helps support and safeguard spiritual growth.

Antonio was a chef extraordinaire. He could pull together ingredients and finesse them into meals that were music on your tongue. Soups filled you with comforting warmth. Salads spoke invigorating health to your body. Pasta dishes silenced conversations, because everyone wanted to experience them so fully.

Antonio's desserts looked so beautiful on the plate you hated to cut into them. But once you did, you couldn't stop eating, the taste was so heavenly. Antonio's specialty was a cake—an extraordinary chocolate cake. It was a symphony of layers and textures and degrees of chocolate that made mouths water at the mere sight of it; in one documented case, a known chocolate lover swooned at the first bite.

One October, Antonio decided to enter his chocolate cake in a statewide contest. He sequestered himself in his kitchen and baked his heart out. When finished, Antonio carefully loaded the cake into his car and drove it to the contest site. As he walked into the room with his cake, a hush fell over the crowd. Here and there, you could hear a muted gasp or a sigh of delight; otherwise, everyone silently beheld Antonio's work of art. Smiling proudly, he walked the cake over to its designated spot and set it down for display.

It was beautiful. It was stunning. Its presentation was flawless.

There was, however, one problem. It tasted awful. The judges, who had looked forward to sampling Antonio's cake, took one bite and grabbed for their water glasses, grimacing in shocked displeasure. To this day, Antonio isn't sure how it happened—whether it was his excitement, his nerves, or a brief lapse in concentration. But he apparently had left out his most important ingredient. *The* ingredient—the one that pulled all the other ingredients together into delectable harmony—was missing.

With one bite, the cake went from a thing of beauty to an utter disappointment. What could have had a blue ribbon instead fell far short of placing. And the crowd of people went away, shaking their heads at what could have been.

Even amazingly beautiful things can leave a bad taste in your mouth—if the key ingredient is missing. It's true in the realm of cooking. It's true when you use your gifts in ministry. The gifts God has given you are beautiful, amazing, a symphony of possibilities. Use them well, and lives will be changed for the better—your life and the lives of those around you. But leave out the key ingredient, and disappointment is inevitable. You can pour all kinds of effort into exercising your gifts, but you will end up with nothing. And, you will leave others with a bad taste in their mouth.

Listen to the apostle Paul talk about the key ingredient:

If I speak in the tongues of men and of angels, but do not have love, I am only a resounding gong or a clanging cymbal. If I have the gift of prophecy and can fathom all mysteries and all knowledge, and if I have a faith that can move mountains, but do not have love, I am nothing. If I give all I possess to the poor and give over my body to hardship that I may boast, but do not have love, I gain nothing. (1 Corinthians 13:1–3)

Your gifts are wonderful. Your gifts are beautiful and vital to the community of believers. But the love factor is the essential ingredient that makes all the other factors work together.

Love a person, and he or she will embrace your gifts, embrace you, embrace your God. Show disregard for a person, and he or she will refuse your gifts, keep you at arm's length, and perhaps even reject your God. The stakes are high. That's why it is so important to be a conduit of God's love before you use your gifts, while you use them, and even afterward. We need to regularly examine the focus of the love in our hearts.

This week, we are going to do just that. We will take a look at various pitfalls we can stumble into as we use the gifts God has given us. As you read, check to see if any pitfall is present in your life. And notice how each one violates the rule of love.

Remember what Jesus said would be the mark of his followers? He didn't say, "Everyone will know you are my disciples by your giftedness." Jesus said, "By this everyone will know that you are my disciples, if you love one another" (John 13:35).

LANDMARK 22:

# Faulty Focus

Have you ever watched children open Christmas presents? They rip off the paper in frenzied enthusiasm. With their first glimpse of the prized toy, their faces light up, and they jump around excitedly and joyously laugh.

Then, with most every child, one of two scenarios happens. (1) The child immediately turns to the person who gave the toy and bowls the giver over with a giant bear hug and a volley of thank yous. Throughout the day, the child returns to the giver at random moments to again express thanks. And the child can't wait to share the amazing new toy with anyone who would enjoy it. Or, (2) the child becomes so immersed in the gift that he or she cannot pull attention away from it to acknowledge the person who gave it. So focused is the child on trying out the new toy that he or she ignores all the other people at the Christmas gathering. And if any of the other children (or adults) approach and ask to try out the toy, the child rudely pushes them away and returns to playing with the toy.

Have you ever watched Christians receive wonderful spiritual gifts from God? The same two scenarios can play out. The believer either takes great joy in the gift but keeps the focus and gratitude aimed toward the giver, or the believer becomes absorbed in the gift itself and loses sight of the one who gave it. As a result, he or she either shares the gift freely with others or hoards it, forgetting the purpose for which the gift was given.

In C. S. Lewis' novel *The Great Divorce,* people take a bus ride from hell to heaven, where they're given the opportunity to stay if they choose. The decision is never as easy as you might think, and the story of each bus rider gives us an insight into the struggles of our own souls.

One person on the bus is a painter. When he steps off the bus in heaven, he immediately wishes he had his painting supplies so that he could paint the beauty he sees. But one of the inhabitants of heaven confronts the painter and tells him there is no need. On earth the painter saw bits of heaven reflected in creation, and through his art, he had helped others see them too. But now the painter has heaven itself, with no need to rely on momentary glimpses to see the beauty.

Faced with choosing between heaven itself and the opportunity to paint small glimpses of it—forced to choose between his gift and the giver of the gift—the painter gets back on the bus. How sad. How foolish. How familiar. Don't we all sometimes hold on to the things God has given us more tightly than we hold on to God? When we do so, we commit our own version of idolatry, breaking the first commandment, which calls us to have no gods but God alone.

One of the saddest passages in the Bible talks about the tragic choice we too often make in the handling of our lives, our possessions, our gifts:

> For although they knew God, they neither glorified him as God nor gave thanks to him, but their thinking became futile and their foolish hearts were darkened. Although they claimed to be wise, they became fools. . . . They exchanged the truth about God for a lie, and worshiped and served created things rather than the Creator—who is forever praised. Amen. (Romans 1:21–22, 25)

Open your spiritual gift and let your face light up. Feel the excitement, and be joyously happy. Then turn immediately to the one who gave you the gift; embrace him, and give him your thanks. Trade the joy of your relationship with the giver for nothing—not even for the joy of the gift he has given to you.

LANDMARK 23:

# Not My Cup of Tea

"I'd love to help, but I don't want to get my hands dirty."

"Sure, I'll clean—but I don't do windows."

"I'm not very good at that. Couldn't you find someone else to do it?"

"Sorry, that's just not my cup of tea."

We've all heard people say these things. We've all said them ourselves. Sometimes it's completely legitimate to say no to an opportunity that presents itself. But most of us can sense the difference between a legitimate, good-hearted no versus a no that stems from

- laziness
- the desire to shirk a responsibility
- the belief that "I'm above doing that sort of task"
- the refusal to do anything that "I'm not really good at"

The truth is that one advantage of knowing your spiritual gifts is that you can evaluate various ministry opportunities and say yes to the ones that are a good fit for you and your gifts and say no to the ones that aren't. But it's also true that participating in a ministry that fits your gifts doesn't give you an exemption from helping other ministries when needed.

God generally calls us to a primary ministry based on our gifts. He may also call us to a secondary ministry, one for which we are not gifted, but we are qualified. Maybe your primary ministry is hosting a small group in your home. You love doing it. You have a passion for seeing people connect in relationships, and you enjoy providing a welcoming place for that to happen. But you also have a junior-high-aged daughter; even though youth ministry is not your passion, you feel God prompting you to participate at various times in youth group activities.

Never does the Bible say to *only* minister with your gifts. Rather, it seems that all of us are called to grow in many areas of ministry—to develop a wide range of ways to reach out to both believers and unbelievers. That's not meant to be drudgery; it is meant to be a stretching, growing opportunity—and a chance to see God at work in wonderful ways outside of our comfort zones. Some of the most amazing tastes of God's grace happen when we follow his calling to serve him in an unfamiliar arena.

Some people are gifted evangelists (Ephesians 4:11). But we are all called to share our faith with others when the opportunity arises: "But in your hearts revere Christ as Lord. Always be prepared to give an answer to everyone who asks you to give the reason for the hope that you have. But do this with gentleness and respect" (1 Peter 3:15).

Some believers have the gift of wisdom (1 Corinthians 12:8). But we are all called to be wise: "Everyone has heard about your obedience, so I rejoice because of you; but I want you to be wise about what is good, and innocent about what is evil" (Romans 16:19).

> God gives some believers gifts of exhortation (Romans 12:8). But we are all called to come alongside and help those who are struggling: "And we urge you, brothers and sisters, warn those who are idle and disruptive, encourage the disheartened, help the weak, be patient with everyone" (1 Thessalonians 5:14).
>
> God gifts some believers with supernatural mercy and compassion toward others (Romans 12:8). But we are all called to "be merciful, just as your Father is merciful" (Luke 6:36).

So, teachers, go serve some punch. Helpers, go tell someone about Jesus. Prophets, go show someone mercy. Administrators, go help in the nursery. Wash some windows. Get your hands dirty. Drink deeply of something that is not your cup of tea. And get ready—you may taste it and see that the Lord is good in ways you haven't known before.

# LANDMARK 24:
# Lazybone Jones and Stickyhands Smith

This here's a short story 'bout two silly folks
(and if it weren't so true, it'd make a good joke).
This here's a brief story 'bout Smith and 'bout Jones
(although when we're not careful, the story's our own).

Lazybone Jones was—well, he was just like his name.
He thought any exertion would cause severe pain.
And so, though there were things that he could have done,
he sat—till his chair conformed to his buns.

And he sat and he sat (just how long I don't know)
until one day his living room started to glow,
and just as his favorite show went to commercial
Jesus appeared (to break Lazy's inertia).

Jesus seemed to have something he wanted to say,
but a deafening soda ad got in the way.
Jones tried to read Jesus' lips and understand.
(Grabbing the remote would take moving his hand.)

Jesus took care of that little hitch in a flash.
A lightning bolt went through the TV with a crash.
Jesus said: "It's high time that we talked and caught up."
(Lazybone was so shocked that he *almost* got up.)

"I gave you a gift once—ain't seen it since."
"It's back in my closet," Lazy said with a wince.
He felt a bit sheepish, and tried to look away.
His chair didn't feel quite so comfy that day.

"A nice gift," said Jesus. "In case you forgot,
it came with instructions to use it a lot.
Consider this just a heavenly reminder—
most gifts can't be used sitting in a recliner.

"What happened, Lazybone, to the plans that we shared,
back before you got mired in your too-comfy chair?
What came of the passion I placed in your soul—
the fire that burned in your heart like a coal?"

Stammered Jones, "I thought that the whole thing could
    wait.
I never realized it might be too late."
("Mañana" was Lazybone's mantra du jour—
and had been since April 1984.)

Jesus made short work of that unfortunate myth,
and before he left Jones to see Stickyhands Smith,
Jesus pulled Lazybone off his derriere,
and together they danced 'round his vacated chair.

Stickyhands Smith was—well, like her name, too—
whatever she acquired stuck with her like glue.
Her house was crammed full, to the tiniest niche,
but the thought of sharing it gave her a twitch.

Sticky had great things, and was glad she possessed them.
She counted them, dusted them, stroked and caressed them.
So this might not surprise you: one day she woke up
to find her fingertips replaced by ten suction cups.

"Well, it's all the better to hold you, my pretties,"
Sticky said to her stuff, and sang loving ditties
while fastening things to her funky new digits.
(Jesus, of course, picked this moment to visit.)

Sticky's left thumb sported her bagpipes (red plaid),
while six fingers displayed her favorite do-dads.
One finger held a book on medical sciences,
and two were bedecked with kitchen appliances.

Again came the glow (like to Jones just before),
and rich light surrounded Stickyhands and her store.
Thinking it might be a thief or a . . . ghost or—
Sticky swung 'round clubbing Christ with a toaster.

Once she recognized her guest as divine,
Sticky apologized, "The fault is all mine!"
Christ shook his head, lying down flat,
"What you've done with your gifts hurts me far more
    than that."

Jesus sighed, looked around, and then shook His head
(and Stickyhands felt stirring a wee sense of dread).
"But Jesus, I've taken such good care of them, see?
I've loved every gift that You've given to me!"

Jesus said, "Your gifts are to enjoy, yes it is true.
But I never meant for their worth to stop here with you.
I gave you those hands to reach out and be kind—
not to see how much you could hold at one time."

Said Jesus, "Stickyhands, please understand.
You've got to loosen your grip to take hold of My hand."
"I'd like to," she said, and shook her paws all around.
But all she created was a cacophonous sound.

The grip of the suction cups couldn't be broken:
the toaster clanked against a plate from Hoboken
and a brooch and a lamp and a set of car keys
and five other things—Sticky cried, "Help, Jesus! Please!"

Again lightning flashed with a *Zim!* And a *Zop!*
and Stickyhands felt the ten suction cups pop.
Her hands were now free; Jesus took them and smiled,
then ran outside to take the breeze, free and wild.

While Jesus headed off to a teen in Toronto,
our heroes got working—speedy and pronto!
It's a fine little story, a true little myth,
so learn from Lazybone Jones and Stickyhands Smith:

You weren't made to snooze and leave gifts on a shelf
or hoard all your gifts—keep them all to yourself.
So if life seems stale—if you'd like one that's finer—
Let go of your grip and get off your recliner.

---

### LANDMARK 25:
# Disorderly Conduct

Smack dab in the middle of a lengthy discussion on the use—and abuse—of spiritual gifts within church gatherings, the apostle Paul made a statement about the character of God—one short, simple statement. But it is amazing how one little sentence can wrap itself around a whole argument and give it greater strength. Paul said, "For God is not a God of disorder but of peace" (1 Corinthians 14:33).

Creation has order: kingdom, phylum, class, order, family, genus, and species. Day follows night; spring follows winter. The planets stick to their orbits, and the stars continue in their constellations century after century. There is security in the consistent laws of nature, which point to the faithfulness of the Creator.

This is what Paul was pointing out in the passage above: the way we use our gifts when we come together can reflect the peace and order of God's character, or it can create an unholy dissonance—a divide between the character of God and the character of those in whom God dwells.

In this passage, Paul talked specifically about times when the entire church gets together—you might think of it as your congregation's weekend service. And he specifically addressed what are often called the "sign gifts": tongues, interpretation of tongues, prophecy. But the principles he applied to these specific situations may also be good guides for smaller groups—and for the rest of the gifts. Are you using your gifts in accordance with these principles?

- Exercising my gift should add to—not detract from—the flow of what God is doing in the gathering.
- I am responsible for evaluating whether what I am experiencing is meant to be a private encounter between God and me, or if it's meant to be shared with the group.
- I am responsible for asking God not only *if* an insight or prompting is to be shared but also *when* it is to be shared.
- The exercise of my gift is subject to confirmation—or rejection—by other mature, Spirit-filled members of the body.
- The use of my gift should draw people closer to God—not scare them away from him.

- Using my gift should always be an act of love—both for God and for the other believers present.

God's Spirit can blow where he pleases (John 3:8). He can (and often does) work in amazing, unexpected, and seemingly spontaneous ways when believers get together. But God's Spirit will never work in a way that contradicts the character of God. He will never create disarray, disorder, or division; God is not a God of disorder, but of peace.

Because we are his followers, our gatherings should reflect God's character and be an oasis of love, order, and peace in a chaotic world.

## LANDMARK 26:
# The Love Test

We often hear 1 Corinthians 13 quoted at weddings. But this description of love actually falls in the middle of a lengthy discussion of how we are to exercise our spiritual gifts in the community of believers.

So for a few minutes, erase the wedding pictures from your mind and replace that scenario with a picture of your particular church. Think of a weekend service, or think of a ministry team you work with or a small group you're a part of.

Can you see the people? Can you see yourself there? Now picture some of the ways God might call you to use a spiritual gift in that group. And, just for practice, put the exercise of your gifts through the love test—what Paul called "the most excellent way," the way of order and of peace. Run your gifts through 1 Corinthians 13:4–7 and see how this test—this pledge—will save you from falling into the pitfalls we have explored.

- ❑ **Love is patient.** Even though God has given me the gift of discernment, I will not assume that I must share every discerned truth immediately.

- ❑ **Love is kind.** Before I exercise the gift of prophecy, I will make sure my motivation is the kindness of God that leads to repentance—not my own indignation at the sin I see.

- ❑ **It does not envy.** I will not allow envy of another person's gift to take root in my heart and cause a rift between God and me, between another believer and me.

- ❑ **It does not boast.** I will not look for opportunities to brag of the ways God has used me so that others will see me as "spiritual," "mature," or "fruitful." I'll let God take care of my reputation.

- ❑ **It is not proud.** Even though God has given me the gift of teaching, I will discipline myself to learn from others. Even though God has given me the gift of helps, I will also let others serve me. Even though God has given me the gift of tongues, I will not think myself to be closer to God than are those with other gifts.

- ❑ **It does not dishonor others.** I will not interrupt someone to exercise my gift. I will not disregard others' feelings to exercise my gift. I will not be disruptive in exercising my gift.

- ❑ **It is not self-seeking.** I will remind myself that my gift of leadership was given not to increase my glory, but to shepherd God's people in humility and love.

- ❑ **It is not easily angered. It keeps no record of wrongs.** I will be patient with myself and with others as we learn together how to use our gifts in community. I will practice forgiveness when mistakes are made.

- **Love does not delight in evil, but rejoices with the truth.** I will not allow my gift of mercy to keep me from confronting a fellow believer about sin when God leads me to humbly do that.

- **It always protects.** I will do my part to make every gathering a safe place for my fellow believers to use the gifts God has given them.

- **Always trusts.** I will trust God to bless me through other believers and to bless other believers through me. I will trust other believers to allow God to bless me through them.

- **Always hopes.** I will hold on to the belief that God has good plans for his gifts in you—and in me.

- **Always perseveres.** I will never let go of the belief that God's character can be reflected in our church. Amen.

## REST STOP

Spend time in prayer today. Ask God to reveal to you the opportunities you have to discover and use your gifts in community with others.

—— 5 ——

# USE WHAT YOU'VE GOT

Discovering your spiritual gift is not a matter of personal preference. The body of Christ is counting on you! God has positioned you in a special place in his plan, in his timing. Think about the human body for just a moment. The elbow is connected to the arm, which is connected to the wrist, which is connected to the hand, which is connected to the fingers—these parts work together. If you take one part away, the other parts can't do their jobs. If you've ever injured your shoulder muscle, you know how that injury can affect even the simplest of tasks such as waving hello to someone. Similarly, as a Christian, you are interconnected with other Christians—and the body of Christ needs you to properly function.

God tells us in 1 Peter 4:10, "Each of you should use whatever gift you have received to serve others." When you read the word *serve,* think of the word *ministry.* Whenever a church talks about ministries of the church or encourages you to "be involved in ministry," they're talking about serving. Ministry is serving God with your life. So, receive your gift in ministry to serve others, "as faithful stewards of God's grace in its various forms." This means that God wants you to faithfully administer to others what he has built into your life.

Romans 12:1 says, "Therefore, I urge you, brothers and sisters, in view of God's mercy, to offer your bodies as a living sacrifice, holy and pleasing to God—this is your true and proper worship." We need to offer ourselves to God in gratitude for his mercy. We were separated from God because of our sin, and we deserved eternal hell. But our merciful God sent his Son Jesus to take our punishment on the cross and graciously adopt us into his family. God lavished on us his mercy, his grace, and his love.

Therefore, in view of God's incomparable gift of his Son, Paul told us to offer our redeemed bodies to this merciful God as an act of worship. We should devote our lives to sacrificial living and to pleasing this gracious God who loves us so much. Ministry—serving God and others—is not an optional experience in the plan of God!

Many of us are tempted to treat the Christian life as though we are buying a car with options. The standard model is, "Look, I want to be a Christian. I want to be in relationship with God and connect my heart to God's heart." Yet we view Christian responsibilities as optional features. Take, for example, being in accountability relationships with other believers in the context of a caring community. "No thanks," we say. "I don't want that option." When viewing features such as giving sacrificially of our time, talent, and our treasure, we say, "Oh, the money thing? What are those people talking about? That's definitely optional." Features such as serving in ministry to others are met with attitudes such as, "Serving? No thanks. No time. That's optional."

If you think that serving God with your life is an optional part of the Christian experience, then you are ignoring core principles. The book of James tells us, "Suppose a brother or a sister is without clothes and daily food. If one of you says to them, 'Go in peace; keep warm and well fed,' but does nothing about their physical needs, what good is it? In the same way, faith by itself, if it is not accompanied by action, is dead" (James 2:15–17).

God created you for a reason. He gave you gifts for a reason. You have a place in God's plan, and if you don't go after that plan, if you don't say, "God, what did you create me to do?" then you will cause the body of Christ to be incomplete.

Fortunately, God has given some very clear lessons in his Word to help us understand his will on the issue of serving him with our lives. In Matthew 25:14–30, Jesus was speaking about our relationship with the Father and about the kingdom of God: "Again, it will be like a man going on a journey, who called his servants and entrusted his wealth to them. To one he gave five bags of gold, to another two bags, and to another one bag, each according to his ability. Then he went on his journey."

Now, let me add a modern twist to the story. Suppose there is a man who owns three business properties. One is a rental property, another is a retail outlet, and the third is a convenience store. Planning a six-month trip out of the country, the man finds his three most-trusted employees and puts each in a position of responsibility over one property while he is gone. Let's continue to read from Scripture: "The man who had received five bags of gold went at once and put his money to work and gained five bags more. So also, the one with two bags of gold gained two more. But the man who had received one bag went off, dug a hole in the ground and hid his master's money."

Let's apply this lesson to our modern version. The man responsible for a property producing $50,000 in revenue doubles the revenue to $100,000. The same happens with the second employee. He receives a property producing $20,000 in revenue; he works hard and doubles that amount to $40,000. But the third man, who is put in charge of the convenience store, is lazy. He does nothing to increase the revenue. Perhaps he even turns out the lights, hoping no customers come into the store. Let's read on:

After a long time the master of those servants returned and settled accounts with them. The man who had received five bags of gold brought the other five. "Master," he said, "you entrusted me with five bags of gold. See, I have gained five more." His master replied, "Well done, good and faithful servant! You have been faithful with a few things; I will put you in charge of many things. Come and share your master's happiness!" The man with the two bags of gold also came. "Master," he said, "you entrusted me with two bags of gold; see, I have gained two more." His master replied, "Well done, good and faithful servant! You have been faithful with a few things; I will put you in charge of many things. Come and share your master's happiness!"

What is the difference between what the master said to the first servant, who doubled five bags of gold, and what he said to the second servant, who doubled two bags? Nothing. This story is not about how many bags of gold each received, but rather what they did with those resources in service to their trusting master. The servant with five bags of gold and the servant with two bags were found faithful. Because of their faithfulness, they received the same affirmation and love from their master and were invited to share in his abundance. Let's read on:

Then the man who had received one bag of gold came. "Master," he said, "I knew that you are a hard man, harvesting where you have not sown and gathering where you have not scattered seed. So I was afraid and went out and hid your gold in the ground. See, here is what belongs to you." His master replied, "You wicked, lazy servant! So you knew that I harvest where I have not sown and gather where I have not scattered seed? Well then, you should have put my money on deposit with the bankers, so that when I returned I would have received it back with interest. So take the bag of gold from him and give it to the one who has ten bags. For whoever has will be given more, and they will have an abundance. Whoever does not have, even what they have will be taken from them. And throw that worthless servant outside, into the darkness, where there will be weeping and gnashing of teeth."

Because of this servant's unfaithfulness, he received condemnation from his master and was removed from the master's presence. This powerful story has significant applications to the way we serve God. There are some pivotal issues here for all of us to take to heart, issues that strike at the core of who we are in relationship with God. Let's look at these principles.

**We are servants of God.** We must ask ourselves, *Who owns my life?* If you believe you own your life, then you most likely do whatever you please—whatever suits your whim. You feel accountable only to yourself. *But* if you believe God owns your life, you will try to make choices that please God. The surprising truth is that as we live for God's pleasure (to give him glory and honor), the Bible says we will experience peace, fulfillment, and joy—the very things we seek but cannot find by pursuing selfish ambitions.

**God entrusts his property and purposes to us.** The God of heaven and earth, who created everything, owns everything in heaven and earth. He is exceedingly generous to share his universe with us and entrust us with his resources. We own nothing—we merely manage his resources for him. This is a humbling realization that should prompt from us gratitude and responsibility.

**God distributes his resources as he wills, not as we demand.** Most of us are probably verbally polite with God. Occasionally, though, I tell him that things down here are all messed up, and I ask him, "When are you going to fix this?" At other times, I feel upset over a lack of resources, relationships, time, or energy, and I pray, "Hey! Fill in the gaps!" But this parable of Jesus teaches us a powerful truth: the Master distributes the resources as he wills, not as we demand.

We really have nothing to do with what gifts God gives us. God gives the resources. Our job is to be grateful and to do all we can to honor him with what we receive.

**We are accountable to God for what we have received.** We all have our own races to run. We are accountable for our own lives, for our personal actions. We are not responsible for taking care of what others have received. This truth helps us stay focused on our own tasks and avoid the pitfall of letting our eyes drift toward others, becoming jealous of what they have received from God.

**There will be a time for settling accounts.** There will be a moment in time when we stand before God and to give an account of our lives. Years ago, I heard Pastor Bill Hybels say, "Someday, you will stand before the nail-pierced hands of your Savior and he will ask you, 'What did you do with the leadership gift I gave you?'" When he said those words, it was as though time stopped, and God pointed his finger at me—not to accuse me, but to remind me. I have a leadership gift, and someday I will have to settle accounts with the God who gave me that gift.

Similarly, I once heard Jack Hayford, pastor of Church on the Way, challenge leaders by saying, "Pastors who do not pray for their churches are guilty of spiritual adultery." Those words shot into my heart like a laser beam, and I just froze. Again God reminded me that I am accountable to him for the calling on my life and for the responsibility he has given me.

Of course, the foremost question asked of us will be, "What did you do with the gift of my Son?" God has offered to us the gift of salvation. Some have not yet received his salvation. They've held it at arm's length or rejected it outright. But for those who have reached out and said yes to Jesus, we are entrusted with kingdom responsibilities—and we will give an account.

**The master expects an increase.** In the story Jesus told, when the master left his resources with his servants, he expected them to take care of those resources and increase his revenue. Similarly, God has given us his resources to expand his kingdom, and he expects us to do so.

**Faithfulness in smaller things results in greater responsibility.** Sometimes, after God has given us an opportunity to use our gifts, we think we deserve a long break when that assignment is completed. In the parable, however, the master complimented the hard-working servants—then he gave them other assignments with even more responsibility.

When we are faithful with a little, God gives us more. Whether we serve two people or two hundred or two thousand people, we have an audience of only one. Our audience is the Father. We live our lives to give him glory and honor. It is not about us; it is about him. When we are faithful in smaller things, he will give us greater responsibility.

**Great responsibility equals greater joy.** After applauding the first two servants' faithfulness and giving them more responsibility, the master invited them to share in his abundance! God wants us to share in his complete joy, in everything that is his. God has designed the church to work in such a way that when we fill our places in God's plan, we will experience his peace, power, and joy. There is nothing better in life than knowing that we are at the center of God's will and sharing life with him.

**Some people view God as unfair, so they refuse to obey.** Some people, like the third servant with one bag of gold, will say, "Hey! This is not fair. I know how this harsh master operates. He expects me to do all the hard work; then he will take for himself whatever increase I gain." So, this lazy servant buried his bag of gold. He was ungrateful and disrespectful, and he neglected his duty. He knew what was expected of him, but he refused to do it. Many of us are ungrateful for what God has given us, we doubt God's goodness, and we accustom ourselves to patterns of disobedience. We simply refuse to fulfill the purpose for which God designed us.

**Your choice to disobey does not nullify your responsibilities.** God holds all people accountable for their lives. Disobedience leads to regrets, tears, and gnashing teeth. I've had conversations with people in their later stages of life who had taken intentional detours from the path of obedience. When they were twenty or thirty years old they knew what God wanted for them, but they told God no. This led to a lifetime of regret.

Remember, though, we serve a God of second chances. No matter when or how you told God no in the past, you can tell God yes today. When you humbly confess your sins and return to your loving Father, he will flood your soul with forgiveness and kindly lead you on a path of blessing. I've seen people end a thirty-year detour and surrender to God's will. He then transformed their character and nature into something beautiful. God, and God alone, has the power to change a broken and wounded heart. Only God can take a life that has been thrashed and trashed and turn it into a treasure.

**God moves with the movers.** Every time I read this parable, I'm surprised that the master gave the unfaithful servant's bag of gold to the one who already had ten. I believe this means that when we are moving along with God, he blesses our lives with more opportunities and more joy. God is moving with the movers. However, if we refuse to move with God, he will give our refused opportunities to someone who will gladly take them in willing service to the Good Master.

**Those who reject God are cast out of his presence.** It's hard to read the end of the story, where it says, "Throw that worthless servant outside, into the darkness, where there will be weeping and gnashing of teeth." The stakes are high.

Finding your place in God's plan is at the core of what it means to follow God and serve him with your life. This is not optional; it relates to the laws of God. God has laws that will not be violated. For example, the law of sowing and reaping shapes our lives: if we sow goodness and kindness into our character and relationships with people, we will reap goodness and kindness. If we sow destruction and deceit and evil in our lives, we will ultimately reap destruction.

In Galatians 6:7–8, we read this: "Do not be deceived: God cannot be mocked. A man reaps what he sows. Whoever sows to please their flesh, from the flesh will reap destruction; whoever sows to please the Spirit, from the Spirit will reap eternal life." And 2 Corinthians 9:6 adds, "Whoever sows sparingly will also reap sparingly, and whoever sows generously will also reap generously."

Everything you have in life has been entrusted to you by God—your relationships, your physical health, your mental health, your financial capacity, your spiritual gifts, and your place in God's body. You have a place in God's plan, and he wants you to fulfill his purpose for your life. When you do, you will discover his peace and his power. That's the promise of the great adventure!

# No Fine Print

*Each of you should use whatever gift you have received to serve others, as faithful stewards of God's grace in its various forms. (1 Peter 4:10)*

You have to hand it to Jesus. While he talked about the benefits of becoming his disciple, he never hid the heavy cost of following him. He didn't hide the reality in fine print or in a maze of legal mumbo-jumbo. He spelled it out clearly:

- "Then Jesus said to his disciples, 'Whoever wants to be my disciple must deny themselves and take up their cross and follow me'" (Matthew 16:24).
- "Jesus replied, 'No one who puts a hand to the plow and looks back is fit for service in the kingdom of God'" (Luke 9:62).
- "In the same way, those of you who do not give up everything you have cannot be my disciples" (Luke 14:33).
- "If the world hates you, keep in mind that it hated me first. If you belonged to the world, it would love you as its own. As it is, you do not belong to the world, but I have chosen you out of the world. That is why the world hates you. Remember what I told you: 'A servant is not greater than his master.' If they persecuted me, they will persecute you also. If they obeyed my teaching, they will obey yours also" (John 15:18–20).

Jesus told the harsh truth. No beating around the bush here. We also don't want to beat around the bush on the issue of spiritual gifts. We've talked about your place in life and ministry for four chapters. You've explored your passions, your personality, your experiences, and your gifts. Now it's time to talk about using and developing your gifts, not just dabbling in ministry here and there, but forging a lifestyle of using your gifts to influence your world.

Any time you get serious about following Jesus' call on your life, there is a cost. Yes, there is satisfaction, fulfillment, enjoyment, and adventure at deep levels. But if you want to do great things for God, there is a price to be paid.

In this round of reflections, we will talk about developing your gifts and using them over a lifetime. We'll address how you can allow God to create in you the character qualities that lead to lasting fruit in your ministry. We will talk about words that make us squirm, words such as

- surrender
- service
- training
- diligence
- accountability

Don't skip these lessons—tempting though it might be. We are not putting this part in fine print, because if you know the cost up front, you can choose to pay it with joy. This is not because you enjoy the discipline or the pain involved, but because you know that the reward is greater than the sacrifice. Let Jesus himself be your model for this.

> Therefore, since we are surrounded by such a great cloud of witnesses, let us throw off everything that hinders and the sin that so easily entangles. And let us run with perseverance the race marked out for us, fixing our eyes on Jesus, the pioneer and perfecter of faith. For the joy set before him he endured the cross, scorning its shame, and sat down at the right hand of the throne of God. Consider him who endured such opposition from sinners, so that you will not grow weary and lose heart. (Hebrews 12:1–3)

## LANDMARK 28:
# A Beginning Prayer—
# A Look at Surrender

Dear God,

I know that my spiritual gift is just that—a gift. It is not mine in the sense of ownership, but mine only in the sense that you've entrusted it to me for this season of ministry. I know that you are the source of the gift, that I have nothing to do with selecting it or producing it in my life.

But now I'm entering a new season of ministry in my church and my world, and I realize that I'm at a new crossroads of surrender. Even though I'm responsible to use and develop the gift you have provided, I need to surrender all this to you.

Father, I surrender to you the right to choose where this gift is used. I will trust you to direct me to the opportunity that fits me best, even if the opportunity is smaller than I had hoped or larger than I think I can handle, even if it's in an area I would never have imagined. I acknowledge that you know me and love me perfectly, so I will follow your lead.

Lord, I also surrender to you the very process of using this gift. I want this ministry to be an act of worship to you. Paul said, "Therefore, I urge you, brothers and sisters, in view of God's mercy, to offer your bodies as a living sacrifice, holy and pleasing to God—this is your true and proper worship" (Romans 12:1).

I want to offer to you my body—and my abilities, my personality, my gift. When I use them, I pray that my actions will be pleasing to you and that you will receive them as worship.

The results, Lord, I also want to leave in your hands. I am responsible to obey your promptings and to faithfully use what you've given me. But the way people respond is not under my control.

You are the one who draws people to yourself. You are the one who brings forth growth. I surrender the results to you.

Finally, God, I surrender to you all the glory for the great things that will happen. I don't want to take credit for what you have done; I want people to see the good that I do and be moved to praise you for it.

Thank you for all you are doing in me and through me.

Amen.

---

LANDMARK 29:

# The Chainsaw— A Look at Service

The large cottonwood tree in Barry's backyard was in need of a trim. It had some dead branches that had been broken by a recent windstorm. Barry knew he needed to deal with it, but he had been so busy he just hadn't taken the time. One night when Barry arrived home from work, he saw his chainsaw sitting in the middle of the garage floor, preventing him from pulling in his car. His wife had a silent way of making her opinion heard.

The next day, before the temperature got too hot, Barry headed to the backyard with his chainsaw in tow. He tried a few times to climb the tree while holding the saw but was unsuccessful. So, he shimmied up the tree, holding a rope he had tied to the saw. After stringing the rope around a higher branch, Barry pulled the saw to himself and went to work.

Barry first removed the dead branches; then he tried to thin the tree to further improve its appearance. A close inspection revealed that his proficiency with a saw left a lot to be desired. However, from the ground, the tree's appearance met with his wife's approval, so Barry's job was done.

When Lisa was ten years old, her dad left his chainsaw in the backyard to run an errand to the hardware store, forgetting that Lisa's soccer game had been cancelled and that she would be home early. When Lisa's dad returned home, his daughter was on the sofa watching TV—and the hedges in the backyard had all been trimmed.

After punishing his daughter for the obvious, Lisa's parents remarked at her amazing skill with a saw, and at such a young age. From that point on, they let Lisa trim trees and bushes on their ten-acre lot—under very close supervision.

When she was fifteen, Lisa experimented with a dead tree on the edge of their property. Instead of cutting the tree down—her original plan—she chopped off the top and used the chainsaw to shape the six-foot trunk into a grizzly bear sculpture. After staining it with wood stain from an old pail she found in the shed, Lisa showed her parents the results. They both gasped—the bear was stunning. That evening, the phone rang many times as impressed neighbors called about the bear sculpture. Soon Lisa was making a lot of money on the weekends, creating art out of dead trees.

How you use a chainsaw makes all the difference. In the hands of one person, a chainsaw can get the job done, albeit ungracefully (and potentially somewhat dangerously). In the hands of another person, the chainsaw becomes a precision tool that can carve a masterpiece.

How you use your abilities and gifts makes all the difference, too. In the hands of one believer, the gift of leadership is a means to an end, a get-the-job-done method of mobilizing people and making a difference, albeit ungracefully. In the hands of another, the gift of leadership is a precision tool that can create order from chaos and mobilize an army of followers full of energy and positive attitudes. The same is true for any of the spiritual gifts listed in Scripture.

We are certainly called to get the job done. But we are also called to serve others in the process—to help them become the best they can be and to reach their potential in Christ. We are called to get the job done, but we are also called to leave the people around us as sculptures, not as stumps. Ask God to guide you in developing graceful and artful ways of expressing genuine love and concern for the people you serve.

---

## LANDMARK 30:
# The New Car—
# A Look at Training

Josh had never owned a new car before; he'd always bought used cars that worked well and had a good repair history. For the past two years, however, he'd been making plans and saving his money to buy a new car.

Josh had done his research and found the make and model of his dream car. Then, in December, his dream became a reality: his company had performed much better than anticipated and his year-end bonus (together with his savings) enabled him to put a large down payment on a new car, while keeping his payments affordable. As he drove off the lot, Josh's prayer, repeated all the way home, went something like this: "Lord, please don't let anyone run into me!"

Most single guys might be a little embarrassed paying for cloth diapers at the checkout counter, but not Josh. With cloth diapers, he carefully washed, waxed, and polished his car. "Nothing but the best for my car," he would say. He cared for that car meticulously and kept it immaculate.

His work paid off. After a few years, when most new cars have lost that new-car look, Josh's car still stood out in the parking lot. Co-workers teased him about buying an identical new car annually to replace the first one, but they knew the real reason his car still looked sharp and ran well: he kept it in tip-top shape.

Because the spiritual gifts we possess are given to us by God's Spirit—and because they are grace gifts given to us at God's choosing—we might forget that we are responsible for keeping our gifts in tip-top shape.

Coaches in professional sports require players to attend practice, to work out with the team and on their own, and to condition their reflexes. Even the best players in the world develop and hone their gifts on a daily basis—during the off-season as well as during the playing season. Runners stretch before their races. Boxers spend a lot of time in the gym before they step into the ring. Pitchers warm up in the bullpen before heading to the mound.

Why is it, then, that Christians sometimes expect to walk onto the field, so to speak, and use their gifts for God's glory with no pre-game preparation? Why is it that the best sports players in the world do not rest on their laurels, yet believers rarely spend time training for ministry? Why do believers too often neglect the intentional development and honing of their gifts?

We have a responsibility to shape and develop those gifts, to use them diligently for God's glory, and to use them out of gratitude for the opportunity to meaningfully serve our loving Father and his people. We have a responsibility to train for the spiritual race God has called us to run. We are responsible for honing our skills and persevering in the application of our gifts.

Need a training plan? Want to be ready next time God calls you onto the playing field? The following are some ways you can shape, hone, and develop your gifts:

- Remember that you have surrendered your gift back to God. Commit to use your gift in whatever way he calls you to—large or small. Remember, God blesses "small" jobs as much as "large" ones (see Matthew 25:23).
- Spend time in community with other Christians who affirm your gift and hold you accountable for using it.

- Read books and Bible passages about subjects that relate to your gift, or by authors who possess a similar gift mix.
- Ask a mature believer who has the same gift to mentor you.
- Learn all you can about your gift and the ways it's utilized to serve God in ministry.
- Consciously use your gift in some way every day.
- Say no to new ministry opportunities that do not fit well with your gifting (unless God calls you to say yes).
- Pray, and dream (big) with God about ways he might want you to use your gift in the future. What things would need to happen to see that dream come to fruition? How does that affect the way you train? What steps do you need to take now?

## LANDMARK 31:
# The Cruise— A Look at Diligence

Dave had always wanted to take his wife, Laura, on a cruise. Not wanting to wait until retirement to do so, he found a great price on the Internet for a cruise to Canada and Alaska, and he booked the trip. The week before the vacation, his workload at the office was unusually heavy. But he was accustomed to hard work and got through it. After a final flurry of paperwork, Dave made it home, packed his clothes, and he and Laura left for the airport the next morning.

They flew to Washington, where they took a cab to the ship. When he walked on board, Dave instantly felt relaxed. It wasn't just the ice sculptures and the huge buffets calling out to him. It was the ocean air. The entire next day he just sat on the deck, looking out at the open ocean, feeling his muscles relax and his mind unwind.

The cruise featured all kinds of exotic food and drink; Dave and Laura especially enjoyed the breakfast buffet. He tried to keep his exercise routine by going to the gym while on the ship, but with all the great food, he had a hard time staying in shape.

Each evening, Dave and Laura enjoyed dinner and dancing, followed by a featured performer: a comedian, a magician, or a singer. Each morning they slept in, ate a late breakfast, read on the deck, showered, napped, ate lunch, toured around that day's port city, and then cleaned up for more dinner and dancing. *We could get used to this life,* he and his wife thought to themselves.

Dave checked his voicemail twice while away. Not a single issue came up that week—there were no problems to solve! After checking it the second time, he walked downstairs to the Jacuzzi and just sat for an hour, thinking about how wonderful the cruise had been.

Leaving the ship at the end of the week wasn't difficult: Dave was ready to live on land again. On the return flight home, however, he started to feel sluggish. The ocean air was replaced with recycled air on the plane. His pants fit (uncomfortably) tighter. Dave thought, *I feel so lazy.*

When he returned to work the next day, Dave's morning commute sufficiently brought back memories of the hectic week before vacation. The entire first day back seemed to move in slow motion. He had quite a bit of work on his desk, and there were employees he needed to touch base with throughout the day. That was usually no problem, except that Dave found himself in some sort of fog. Everyone else seemed to be moving at a quicker pace. Dave felt blimp-ish and slow.

He took thirty minutes for lunch to eat his sandwich and chips, though afterward, Dave still felt hungry. Two weeks ago this same lunch would have filled me up, he thought. Barely accomplishing a third of what he needed to do that day, Dave left for home, skipping his usual stop at the gym. He just wasn't in the mood.

The next day Dave did make it to the gym, though he lacked the stamina he had before vacation—and before he tipped the scales at nine pounds heavier. That day he accomplished more at work but still felt as if he were in a bit of a fog. Numbers and totals just weren't coming to him quickly. Dave spent his day alternating between wondering when he would be fit again and when he could book another cruise.

Laziness can be addictive. The less we work, the less we want to work—and the more sluggish we may feel when we do start working again. Do we need vacations? Absolutely yes. Vacations are great. But we can't live on the cruise ship.

The same thing happens spiritually. God has wired us with a unique mix of gifts, skills, and experiences. The less often we use all of these things for God's glory, the less often we will want to—and the more sluggish we will feel when we try to start working in ministry again. Do we need to take breaks from programmed ministry now and then? Sure. It is necessary and delightful to refresh our spirits. But we can't take up residence on our spiritual cruise ship, or we will be tempted to sit in the deck chair and watch life and ministry pass us by.

Over and over, the Bible calls us to avoid laziness and to pursue diligence. It challenges us not to neglect our gifts, but to exercise them faithfully. Listen to Paul talk to his friend Timothy:

> Don't let anyone look down on you because you are young, but set an example for the believers in speech, in conduct, in love, in faith and in purity. Until I come, devote yourself to the public reading of Scripture, to preaching and to teaching. Do not neglect your gift, which was given you through prophecy when the elders laid their hands on you. Be diligent in these matters; give yourself wholly to them, so that everyone may see your progress. Watch your life and doctrine closely. Persevere in them, because if you do, you will save both yourself and your hearers. (1 Timothy 4:12–16)

If you want your ministry to be fruitful—if you want to see a great harvest—diligence is one character trait you will need to cultivate. Look at the contrast in results:

- Sluggards do not plow in season; so at harvest time they look but find nothing (Proverbs 20:4).
- Let us not become weary in doing good, for at the proper time we will reap a harvest if we do not give up (Galatians 6:9).

In other words, don't try to live on a cruise ship if you want to be a fisher of men.

LANDMARK 32:
# High Stakes—
# A Look at Accountability

The parable of the bags of gold shows us that God doesn't just let it slide when we don't use our gifts effectively. Apparently, when Jesus returns, there will be a difference in how he responds to the faithful and to the lazy. When God created good works for us to *do* (Ephesians 2:10), he actually expected us to do them!

Yes, God is loving. Yes, he is merciful and forgiving. But he is also just.

> Do not be deceived: God cannot be mocked. A man reaps what he sows. Whoever sows to please their flesh, from the flesh will reap destruction; whoever sows to please the Spirit, from the Spirit will reap eternal life. Let us not become weary in doing good, for at the proper time we will reap a harvest if we do not give up. (Galatians 6:7–9)

A heavy dose of responsibility comes with the gifts God entrusts to us, a striking accountability that goes along with our gifts. God knows something that we often forget: there are high stakes—eternal stakes—attached to our actions. Here are three of them:

1. **Your redemptive potential.** Follow God wholeheartedly, use your gifts faithfully, and you can live as the person God created you to be. When God redeemed you, he had a dream for you. If you bury your gifts, what happens to that dream?

2. **Someone's answer to prayer.** Every day, millions of believers pour out the needs of their hearts in prayer. Every day, God sends people and their gifts as the answers to some of those prayers. If you yield to God's Spirit and use your gifts to minister to others, you can be a holy conduit and the answer to the cry of someone's heart.

3. **Someone's eternal destiny.** People die every day, entering a Christless eternity. How can we neglect our gifts in the face of that reality? We have a holy obligation to use our gifts to love people, to share Jesus' love in a sin-sick world, and to equip the community of believers to reach out to people who need a Savior. Jesus talked about the church being God's plan to redeem the world; he never mentioned a Plan B.

The stakes are high. It is a sobering thought, but an invigorating one too. It reminds us that there is more to life than paying the bills, doing the laundry, or repairing the car. There is a world to be reached. So, who wants to be caught with their gifts buried in the ground when Jesus returns?

# It's Worth It

It's better than a retirement dinner or a gold watch. It's better than a going-away party or embossed stationery.

During transitions, we gather and wish a fond farewell to a friend or coworker who is moving on to a new venture. Sometimes it's a job or a school far away; other times it's retirement after a fruitful career. Toasts are made, an occasional "roasting" occurs, and good wishes are communicated.

Such parties are often filled with joy and tears. One by one, gifts are opened and words of appreciation are shared. Conversation is punctuated by an occasional emotional release or a hug to communicate love and admiration. It's a time to celebrate the impact a person has had in one place or season, before they continue to the next one.

One day we will all attend the ultimate transition party. Believers from all nations will gather at God's throne to worship and to celebrate his work in each of our lives. We will not know until then all the ways God worked in and through us over our lifetime to accomplish his purposes on earth. We will receive commendation from our Master at that time—and we might hear from others as well.

> "Thank you. You might not remember me, but when you let me use your mobile phone outside of the department store that day, your generosity overwhelmed me. My child was locked in the car, and I couldn't leave to find a pay phone. So I prayed and prayed that someone would come by to help. God used you to answer my prayers."

"Thank you. Do you recall the visit you made to the hospital after I had surgery? The card and the flowers were great, but what you said that day stuck with me the rest of my life—when I faced much darker trials than that surgery. Thank you for your ministering words. Let me tell you how God used them to change my heart . . ."

"Thank you. You fed me when I was hungry, when things were at their worst. Do you remember? You had probably given food to hundreds of people, but for me that day was different. You blessed me with food—and you prayed for me. Your prayer really made me think hard about some thing—things that I had buried for years. Life changed radically after that prayer. I mended my relationship with my brother, and we actually started a business together. We were able to employ fifty people and be a blessing to countless customers. Probably none of that would have happened without your love, concern, and prayers. Thank you."

It's going to be better than a retirement dinner. It's going to be better than a going-away party. Infinitely better. Eternally better. We do not have the time, energy, or awareness to keep track of all the ways we've blessed others or been blessed by them. Key moments may stand out, but the day-after-day service to God tends to blur in our minds to eventually be forgotten. But God doesn't forget; one day everything will be brought to light.

Using your gifts in ministry is hard work. It takes surrender, service, training, diligence, and accountability. But it's worth it—just wait and see! The sacrifice is temporary. The rewards are eternal.

*God is not unjust; he will not forget your work and the love you have shown him as you have helped his people and continue to help them. (Hebrews 6:10)*

*Do you not know that in a race all the runners run, but only one gets the prize? Run in such a way as to get the prize. Everyone who competes in the games goes into strict training. They do it to get a crown that will not last, but we do it to get a crown that will last forever. (1 Corinthians 9:24–25)*

# 6

# LET GOD BE THE JUDGE

Unless you're careful, somebody will press you into a mold that doesn't fit you. Unless you're careful, somebody will have you run a race that is not yours to run. Unless you're careful, you will take on an assignment that is not yours. The fact is that God did not make you *average*. You are a perfect fit for the place God has designed especially for you, and he's given you gifts to joyfully fulfill that place.

Let me tell you a story about an animal school.

> Once upon a time, the animals decided they must do something heroic to meet the problems of "a new world." So they organized a school.
>
> They had adopted an activity curriculum consisting of running, climbing, swimming, and flying. To make it easier to administer the curriculum, all the animals took all the subjects.
>
> The duck was excellent in swimming. In fact better than his instructor, but he made only passing grades in flying and was very poor in running. Since he was slow in running, he had to stay after school and also

drop swimming in order to practice running. This kept up until his webbed feet were badly worn and he was only average in swimming. But average was acceptable in school so nobody worried about that, except the duck.

The rabbit started at the top of the class in running but had a nervous breakdown because of so much makeup work in swimming.

The squirrel was excellent in climbing until he developed frustration in the flying class where his teacher made him start from the ground up instead of from the treetop down. He also developed a "charlie horse" from overexertion and then got a C in climbing and D in running.

The eagle was a problem child and was disciplined severely. In the climbing class, he beat all the others to the top of the tree but insisted on using his own way to get there.

At the end of the year, an abnormal eel that could swim exceedingly well, and also run, climb, and fly a little had the highest average and was valedictorian.

The prairie dogs stayed out of school and fought the tax levy because the administration would not add digging and burrowing to the curriculum. They apprenticed their children to a badger and later joined the groundhogs and gophers to start a successful private school. ("The Animal School," by George H. Reavis can be found online at www.surfaquarium. com/presentations/MI.pdf)

Only God judges perfectly. We look at the world through imperfect eyes, through our own flawed perspectives. We make judgments about other people based on our faulty views. We think we have enough information about others to make right judgments, but we don't. We make this mistake in the world and in the church as well.

In 1 Corinthians 4:1–5, the apostle Paul addressed this issue of judging the service of others. The duty of a servant is to manage the master's affairs so that the purposes of the master are realized. A servant must be faithful to the master's trust. The Corinthian believers were being critical of Paul's ministry. He told them that their evaluation of him was irrelevant and that even his own evaluation of his performance may be faulty. What mattered was God's evaluation of his service. Only God has enough information to make accurate judgments. Paul wrote:

> This, then, is how you ought to regard us: as servants of Christ and as those entrusted with the mysteries God has revealed. Now it is required that those who have been given a trust must prove faithful. I care very little if I am judged by you or by any human court; indeed, I do not even judge myself. My conscience is clear, but that does not make me innocent. It is the Lord who judges me. Therefore judge nothing before the appointed time; wait until the Lord comes. He will bring to light what is hidden in darkness and will expose the motives of the heart. At that time each will receive their praise from God.

Paul said there will come a time when we stand before God. It will not be important then what other people think of us—as important as it may seem right now. It will not even be important then what we think of ourselves. What will be important at the end of all time is *what God thinks of us.*

The truth is that we are all common vessels. None of us is fine china. Nevertheless, each of us has been entrusted with God's heavenly treasure. In 2 Corinthians 4:7, Paul remarked how amazing it is that God puts heavenly treasure in ordinary vessels (cracked pots, like you and me). We all have *issues*—yet God places heavenly treasure in us anyway.

God will examine our motives, not our appearance. God sees inside our hearts. He understands our intentions. Whereas we make judgments on the externals of people, God does not. Is the intent of your heart to serve him and to be faithful to him?

In 1 Corinthians 3:10–11, Paul wrote, "By the grace God has given me, I laid a foundation as a wise builder, and someone else is building on it. But each one should build with care. For no one can lay any foundation other than the one already laid, which is Jesus Christ."

In this passage, Paul was talking about establishing the local church in Corinth, where he had laid the foundation on the gospel of Jesus Christ—the only true foundation. Other leaders after Paul continued the spiritual "construction" of the church at Corinth. Paul was warning people to be careful how they built into the local church.

By application, we can take Paul's warning and examine how we are building our own spiritual lives. Like construction workers, we are building our lives on some foundation. Only one foundation lasts for all eternity, that is, the foundation of a relationship with God through Jesus Christ. Sometimes people refer to this lasting foundation as a "crutch." But, everyone has a crutch, whether it's self-reliance, financial success, social position, prestige, or power. So the question is this: On which foundation are you building your life—an eternal foundation or a temporary one?

Paul's warning continued:

> If anyone builds on this foundation using gold, silver, costly stones, wood, hay or straw, his work will be shown for what it is, because the Day will bring it to light. It will be revealed with fire, and the fire will test the quality of each person's work. If what has been

built survives, the builder will receive a reward. If it is burned up, the builder will suffer loss but yet will be saved—even though only as one escaping through the flames. (1 Corinthians 3:12–15)

This passage teaches that it is possible to build on the foundation of Christ using either material, superior or inferior. We can serve God in superior ways or in inferior ways. We can spend our time achieving eternal goals or temporal goals. Paul encouraged believers to build the church using durable materials that would stand the test of the holy fire of the Lord's judgment. In that judgment day, our worthless deeds will be consumed, and we will suffer loss of reward; our eternal deeds will endure the fire, and we will be rewarded accordingly. God will finally expose the work of his servants. No servant will suffer the loss of salvation ("the builder will suffer loss but yet will be saved"), only the loss of reward. So, God wants us to build on the foundation of Christ using superior materials (godly deeds). God wants us to faithfully use in the church the gifts he has given us, for the good of others and for his glory. Then, one day God will judge our construction project—and he will judge perfectly.

Several years ago, I helped a friend do some repair work on a roof. I told my friend, "You know, I'm not very good at this." He replied, "That's OK, I just need an extra pair of hands. All you have to do is carry things and do what I tell you to do. It will be a piece of cake." My friend then picked up a chalk line and said, "Take this end of the chalk line to the other end of the roof; then I'll snap it to make a perfectly straight line." I went to the other side, but at first I didn't hold the line tightly enough. My friend started to get frustrated because he knew that every step of the process was important. An inferior line would result in an inferior roof. When I finally got my end of the line taut, he snapped a straight line, and we began the roofing project.

I never went into the roofing business, but I learned a critical lesson that day. God holds the chalk line of my life in a secure, solid way. He has a project in mind that he has perfectly designed for me. I'm on the other end of the chalk line, but I just might be dawdling around, preventing him from snapping a perfectly straight line for the project. I must hold the line tightly and follow his straight line to complete the project to his approval.

Know this: God loves you and watches over you daily. He is doing a miracle of transformation in your soul. So, grab your end of the chalk line, pull tightly, and follow the straight and narrow line that he snaps, because the miracles that will follow and the fruit you will bear will delight your heavenly Father, the church he established, and you, his beloved child. Whatever your role is in the church—whether you are an elbow or an arm or a wrist or a hand or fingers or an ear or a foot—you are perfectly suited to the treasure he has entrusted to you. One day you will stand before your loving heavenly Father and all your service will be brought to light. Your faithful work will become evident, and you will receive praise for your loyal service.

LANDMARK 34:
# Base Camp

I've never climbed Mount Everest, but I have read a book and a few articles about people who have scaled the world's highest peak. Here, then, is my limited, nonprofessional understanding of how to climb Mount Everest:

1. Train like crazy so that you're in the best physical shape of your life.
2. Gather high-quality supplies and equipment.

3. Show up in Katmandu and then travel to Base Camp.

4. Spend enough time at Base Camp to adjust to the altitude and to prepare yourself, your team, and your equipment.

5. Move toward the summit, taking plenty of oxygen and courage—because you are heading higher than you've ever been in your life.

For several weeks now, we've been companions on a spiritual adventure. We entered into training together, getting ourselves into shape for ministry. We gathered high-quality supplies and equipment: our abilities, passions, desires, experiences, and spiritual gifts. We traveled over much spiritual geography together, and now we have arrived . . . at Base Camp.

The adventure has been great, but it has only just begun. The bigger adventure lies ahead of you.

Consider this final chapter's readings to be a type of Base Camp. Use this opportunity to make sure all your supplies and equipment are accounted for. Spend time with your climbing companions. Take some deep breaths and reflect on what it was (who it was) that called you to this mountain in the first place.

At the end of the week, you will move out of Base Camp with six key principles, and toward the summit. You will head higher than you've ever been in your life. So use these next few days to make sure you are ready. Follow Paul's climbing advice to his protégé, Timothy:

> For this reason I remind you to fan into flame the gift of God, which is in you through the laying on of my hands. For the Spirit God gave us does not make us timid, but gives us power, love and self-discipline. (2 Timothy 1:6–7)

The God who gifted you for the climb ahead has also given you the power, the love, and the self-discipline to reach the summit.

# A Friendly Reminder

**Key Principle 1:** God has designed a unique and important place for you in the world. Find it and you will find a deeper, richer life that fits your distinctive personality, desires, passion, and experience.

*For we are God's handiwork, created in Christ Jesus to do good works, which God prepared in advance for us to do. (Ephesians 2:10)*

Maybe it's not the first thing you think about when you wake each morning and look in the mirror: *Yep. I'm God's handiwork—uniquely designed to do the important work he has prepared for me.* Maybe the bleary eyes and the bedhead get in the way.

We all need to be reminded now and then that God loves us and has designed us to perfectly fit our calling. Hopefully, through these chapters you have explored who God created you to be. Don't let these insights slip away. Let the Holy Spirit remind you of what insights you have had concerning each of the following:

- special traits in my personality
- desires
- passion
- ideas for expressing that passion
- past experiences
- ideas for using my experiences

*Let your light shine before others, that they may see your good deeds and glorify your Father in heaven. (Matthew 5:16)*

# Finding Your Way

**Key Principle 2:** God has given you spiritual gifts. Discovering those gifts equips you to fulfill God's purpose for your life.

*There are different kinds of gifts, but the same Spirit distributes them. There are different kinds of service, but the same Lord. There are different kinds of working, but in all of them and in everyone it is the same God at work. Now to each one the manifestation of the Spirit is given for the common good. (1 Corinthians 12:4–7)*

Whenever I ask someone for directions, I also ask what indicators along the way will let me know I'm on the right track—things such as "You'll pass an elementary school" or "There isn't a street sign, but the house on the corner has a picket fence." Then, when I see the school and the fence, I can breathe a sigh of relief, confident I'm going in the right direction.

Did you ever wish there were indicators that would let you know you are on the right track to fulfill God's purpose in your life? You know that discovering your gifts equips you to fulfill God's purpose for you, but how do you know you're heading in the right direction with those gifts?

The apostle Paul prayed some great prayers in the letters he wrote to New Testament churches. One of those encouraging prayers is found in Colossians. If you read it closely, you might find some good indicators.

For this reason, since the day we heard about you, we have not stopped praying for you. We continually ask God to fill you with the knowledge of his will through all the wisdom and understanding that the Spirit gives, so that you may live a life worthy of the Lord and please him in every way: bearing fruit in every good work, growing in the knowledge of God, being strengthened with all power according to his glorious might so that you may have great endurance and patience, and giving joyful thanks to the Father, who has qualified you to share in the inheritance of his holy people in the kingdom of light. For he has rescued us from the dominion of darkness and brought us into the kingdom of the Son he loves, in whom we have redemption, the forgiveness of sins. (Colossians 1:9–14)

Did you find the indicators? Here are the ones I found, accompanied by an explanation. Ask yourself the questions below to get a good idea whether you are fulfilling God's purpose for you.

**Am I bearing fruit?** Fruitfulness occurs in the convergence of God's Spirit meeting human needs through your ministry. If your ministry is bearing fruit in your heart and in others' hearts, and if you're daily listening to the Holy Spirit guiding your thoughts and actions toward others, you know you are on the right path.

**Am I growing in the knowledge of God?** God has revealed himself through his creation, through the written Word, and through the person and work of Jesus Christ. A growing life is characterized by regularly studying the Bible, alone and in groups, and by doing what the Bible says, while intentionally developing relationships with other Christians in a community of faith.

**Am I depending on God's strength?** If you're serving God and growing in God's Word but find yourself burned out, you may be suffering from a lack of dependence on God's supernatural resources. A life pleasing to God depends on God for strength. Keep turning to God, relying on his strength to accomplish your God-given mission, and trusting him for the results.

**Am I regularly engaged in giving thanks?** God's Word reminds us to rejoice and be thankful in all our circumstances, because God is at work (1 Thessalonians 5:16–18; Romans 8:28). As you grow in awareness that God is always at work for your good and his glory, you will also grow in genuine gratitude for his grace in your life and through your ministry.

You will not reach perfection in these areas this side of heaven. But when you experience the confluence of fruit bearing, growth in knowledge, dependence on God's strength, and thanksgiving, you can be confident you're heading in the right direction—you are fulfilling God's purpose for you in life and ministry.

---

LANDMARK 37:
# Symbol of the Quest

**Key Principle 3:** Your spiritual gifts are a treasure. Embarking on the quest to discover your gifts can pull you into the adventure of a lifetime—even of an eternity.

> *The kingdom of heaven is like treasure hidden in a field. When a man found it, he hid it again, and then in his joy went and sold all he had and bought that field. (Matthew 13:44)*

Many adventurers carry with them some symbol of their quest or of the one who sent them on the journey—a flag, a crested shield, a memento.

- Knights carried their lady's handkerchief as they entered a jousting competition.
- Moses carried a staff.
- Luke Skywalker carried Obi-Wan Kenobi's light saber.
- Elisha wore Elijah's cloak.
- Columbus flew the flag of Ferdinand and Isabella.

- Frodo wore the ring on a chain around his neck.
- Little leaguers often choose a jersey number that matches their baseball hero's number.

There is power in a symbol. That's why adventurers carry them. That's why God uses them so often in the lives of his people. Consider Passover, communion, and baptism.

Spend some time today in thought and prayer. As you embark on the adventure to discover and use your spiritual gifts, what symbol of your quest would you like to carry with you? If you were to design a flag, what would it look like? If you were to wear a necklace, what sort of pendant would hang from the chain? If you were to choose a uniform, what would it be?

And what exactly does your symbol represent to you? Does it bring to mind the one who called you to the adventure? The gifts he has given to you? The ministry you are pursuing? The people you hope to touch?

Emblazon your symbol so clearly in your mind that you'll be able to summon the image when you need strength on your journey. If possible, make or acquire the object you have imagined so that you can have an actual, physical reminder of your quest.

LANDMARK 38:

# Heaping Supply of Love

**Key Principle 4:** Spiritual growth happens in community. Discovering your gifts within a community of faith helps to support and safeguard spiritual growth.

*A new command I give you: Love one another. As I have loved you, so you must love one another. By this everyone will know that you are my disciples, if you love one another." (John 13:34–35)*

Now that you've studied, prayed, and reflected on your gifts and the amazing place you have in God's plan, it's time to practice loving service in your church and in your world. Here are some ways to get started in your spheres of influence.

## In Your Workplace or School

- Write down the names of every person with whom you have regular contact. Beside each name, make notes of key dates, major issues they are facing, and ways you can love them with the love of Christ.
- Write down the names of those who directly supervise you, if applicable. Pray for them daily, and make an effort in your work to serve them in ways that facilitate their success.
- Write down the names of those you directly oversee, and ask them what specifically you can do to help them succeed in their work.

## In Your Local Community

- Pray every day for a week as you read the local paper. Ask God to reveal the needs of the community that are close to his heart.
- Briefly interview a handful of local journalists, elected officials, and clergy. Tell them you plan to volunteer your time in the community, and ask what they perceive to be the community's greatest need.
- Walk through the neighborhoods near your work, school, or home. Pray for the residents living there, and ask God

to bring to mind issues and needs that can be met in Jesus' name.

## In Your Local Church

- Pray for the children, youth, and adults who attend each weekend and participate in ministries throughout the week. Ask three or four committed lay leaders what they perceive to be the greatest needs in the church.
- Pray for the pastors of your church daily. Ask God to bless them with wisdom, integrity, depth, and fruitfulness.
- Volunteer in two ministries that need participants. Think of your service as twofold: an area of primary service in a key zone of your spiritual gift mix, and a secondary area of service in an area with a significant need.
- Try to balance your volunteer time between the local church ministry (which will enhance the church's impact in the community) and the community (which will shed the light of Christ's love in parts of your community your church may not be touching).
- When you volunteer to serve, follow through and do it joyfully. If you simply cannot serve in a particular opportunity, say no without feeling one ounce of guilt.

## In Your Neighborhood

- Take good care of your front yard.
- Write down the names of the people who live closest to you. If you live in a row of houses, commit to meeting and knowing people in the three homes on your left, three homes on your right, and four homes across from you.
- Spend time in your front yard, and regularly greet and speak with your neighbors on the weekends.

- Take meals or baked goods to your neighbors on key holidays and significant moments in their lives (Christmas, weddings, funerals, birthdays, parties).
- Pray for opportunities to love your neighbors with the love of Christ.
- Contact your church office to ask if other church members live on your street (ask for *nonconfidential* information). Meet those neighbors, and team up in creative ways to build a sense of community on your street.

---

## LANDMARK 39:
# Cultivation

**Key Principle 5:** Each of us is responsible to develop the gift that God has given us. The body of Christ is counting on us! Faithfully develop your gifts; then watch God open doors of opportunity for you, ones you never would have imagined.

> *Each of you should use whatever gift you have received to serve others, as faithful stewards of God's grace in its various forms.*
> *(1 Peter 4:10)*

Some plants grow with no maintenance; they're called weeds. To grow something good, we generally have to care for it: water it, check its light exposure, provide good soil and fertilizer, prune it when needed—the list goes on.

To cultivate the gifts God has given you takes care as well: you have to engage in surrender, service, training, diligence, and accountability. God may have planted some idea-seeds within you about how you might develop your gifts by ministering in your various spheres of influence. Now it's time to water those seeds.

Pray before you begin this project, and plan to refer to the project at least weekly to see how you're progressing.

————————————

LANDMARK 40:
# Epilogue

**Key Principle 6:** God has designed a unique and important place for you in the world. Enter into your calling with confidence and a commitment to use well the treasure he has entrusted to you.

*For this reason I remind you to fan into flame the gift of God, which is in you through the laying on of my hands. For the Spirit God gave us does not make us timid, but gives us power, love and self-discipline. (2 Timothy 1:6–7)*

Take a few minutes to read the stories from Landmark 1 again. Remember the square peg, the child, and the bull? Bring them to your imagination. You might have wondered how their stories ended. Here are the conclusions to their tales.

The square peg grew to love the square hole where the carpenter had placed him. For the first time, he felt secure in his calling. He felt a passion to fill the gaps around him—and he knew, based on his shape, that he could do so. With joy and energy, he sprang out of bed each morning, raring to go. Satisfaction and fulfillment sent him to bed each night with the happy fatigue of one who had lived the day well.

He loved his work. As time went by, the square peg discovered that even deeper than his love for his work was his love for the carpenter who had created him, who had designed the place where he lived. The square peg felt no greater joy than when the carpenter sat down and the two of them talked. The square peg's greatest boast was knowing the carpenter, the one who shared his work and his heart with the square peg. The square peg had no greater amazement than when the carpenter picked him up one day, and the peg realized he had become shaped not only to his hole but also to the carpenter's hand. He loved the carpenter.

-------

The child, meanwhile, danced with newfound freedom. The music she heard grew ever stronger and her steps ever more sure. The tears that ran down her face were now tears of joy. Life was so full inside her it couldn't help but leak out. Her jubilant grace and energy and beauty danced hope into people's lives. The child's heart thrilled to see the despondent learn to move to the rhythm of delight. The child loved the dance.

As time went by, the child discovered that even deeper than her love for the dance was her love for the drummer whose music she heard. The child felt no greater joy than when she joined hands with the drummer and the two of them danced and spun and leaped to the rhythm of the music they shared. The child's greatest boast was knowing the drummer, the one who shared his heart and his dance with her. And the child had no greater amazement than when she practiced one day in front of a mirror and realized that her dance looked more and more like his. She loved the drummer.

-------

The bull, now living in the wide-open spaces he was created for, had grown more comfortable with the power that coursed through his frame. With plenty of room outdoors for his energy and drive, the bull's leaps grew ever longer, his running ever faster. He gathered around himself a herd—animals that heard his passion and his call and followed him deeper into the wild.

The bull loved his freedom. As time went by, the bull discovered that even deeper than his love for freedom was his love for the lion who had freed him. The bull felt no greater joy than when the lion joined him for a wild run through a threatening storm, the wind whipping against their faces, almost taking their breath away. The bull's greatest boast was knowing the lion, who shared his heart and his passion with the bull. The bull had no greater amazement than seeing reflected in a quiet pond that the expression in his eyes looked more and more like the lion's. He loved the lion.

There is joy and jubilance and freedom in the calling. But the greatest joy is this: when the calling is heeded truly with faithfulness and diligence, it leads you back to the one who called you. And you fall more deeply in love with him. Your greatest boast is that you know your Savior; your greatest amazement is that through the ministry he has given you, your heart is being formed to look more and more like his.

# DISCUSSION GUIDE
## FOR GROUPS, CLASSES, AND MINISTRY TEAMS

### Session 1: Welcome to the Adventure!

#### Key Principle

God has designed a unique and important place for you in the world. Find it and you will find a deeper, richer life that fits your distinctive personality, desires, passion, and experience.

#### Note to Leaders

Thank you for taking on the leadership of a group, class, or ministry team! You are playing a critical role in the lives of all who attend your group. Remember to pray for your group daily, and remember each person by name.

You set the tone for the whole adventure at this first meeting. Make sure you're genuinely welcoming and enthusiastic, looking forward to what God will do.

Keep in mind that new people may come to your group or class. Go out of your way to welcome them, and thank them for coming. At the first session, have people sign up to bring food and drink to each of the next five sessions.

In session two, there is an opportunity for a group member to share his or her testimony. Think about whom you will ask to share.

### To Begin

In the daily readings from the first few days of the adventure (chapter one), what has struck you so far? Did you find yourself thinking a lot about a particular point or wrestling with a concept? If so, what? How did God speak to you?

Go around the group with introductions. Share your name, where you were born, how long you've lived in the area, and how long you've attended the church.

### Play a Game: Two Truths and a Lie

Have group members write on a piece of paper two things about themselves that are true and one that is not. Have a member read his or her three statements aloud. As a group, try to guess which statement is not true. Continue with each group member.

### Session Purpose
- To meet other members of the spiritual adventure
- To begin the spiritual adventure as a group
- To challenge participants with regular attendance at the group sessions and the weekend services

- To introduce the topic: gifts and finding your niche in life and ministry

## Diving In

Have you ever felt out of place? Have you ever attended an important function dressed inappropriately? How did that experience feel? Did you take steps to fit in?

## For Study and Discussion

"Some of us feel stuck in a job, in a ministry, in a life that just doesn't seem to fit us. We are square pegs stuck in a round hole. We've been there so long we've resigned ourselves to it. We've lost all hope that there might actually be a hole, the *right*-shaped hole, where *our* shape fits exactly" (from the daily readings, Landmark 1).

When you think about your job, your ministry to others, and your service in the community, have you ever resigned yourself to not finding your niche? When? What was that like? How does it feel to be in the right niche?

Read Psalm 139:13–16.

1. How often do you feel "fearfully and wonderfully made"? Who was the first person in your life to treat you as though you were a highly valuable treasure?

2. Since we know that God doesn't make junk, what should we do when we start to feel as if we are junk?

Read Romans 8:28 aloud as a group. Then get together with one partner in your session to talk about the following:

1. an experience in my past I would like to see God use for good

2. something I've felt passionately about lately that I would like to see God use for good

3.  something I am discovering about my personality that I would like to see God use for good (see Landmark 4 for help in discovering basic attributes of your personality)

Read Galatians 5:13–15.

1.  What is the primary challenge in these verses? If you had to boil it down into a one-word command, what would that word be? Why is this so important to God?

2.  What barriers keep you from finding your place in life and ministry? What barriers from the following list keep you from diving into a ministry?
    - people ("I've been hurt before")
    - knowledge ("I do not know how")
    - schedule ("I am very busy")
    - desire ("I do not want to")
    - other _____

3.  What would it take to remove the barriers you face?

## The Challenge

Write on a piece of paper the painful experiences from your past you think God may want to redeem and turn into opportunities to minister to others. Then write down other experiences from your past you think God may also use: educational experiences, training you've received, spiritual experiences, and past ministry experiences. Begin praying about ways God might use those experiences to minister to other people.

## Before Next Time

Commit to reading each day in the daily devotions and attending church each weekend during the spiritual adventure. Make reading and prayer time part of your daily routine. Start praying now about how God might change your life in and through the adventure.

# Session 2: You've Got Gifts

## Key Principle
God has given you spiritual gifts. Discovering those gifts equips you to fulfill God's purpose for your life.

## Session Purpose
- To cover the basics of spiritual gifts—the who, what, where, why, and when
- To understand and apply the principle of surrendering our lives and gifts to God

## Note to Leaders
Remember that the groups, classes, and teams are not closed to others. Encourage individuals in your group to invite new people to join you.

In this session, your group will dialogue about their experiences with spiritual gifts. Steer the conversation away from debate, and help draw out the positive and negative experiences group members have had.

## To Begin
What struck you from the daily readings in this chapter? What did you find yourself thinking about or wrestling with? How did God speak to you?

## Testimony
Have someone in your group share how they came to place faith and trust in Jesus Christ. Ask them before your group meets to prepare a 3- to 4-minute testimony on how God worked in them

before coming to faith, during the salvation experience, and in daily life now as a Christian.

## Diving In

Has anyone ever forgiven a debt (of money, a favor, a gift, a meal) that you owed, even though you did not deserve to be forgiven? How did it feel to be released from that debt?

On a whiteboard or large piece of paper, write down everything that comes to mind from the group when they hear the term *spiritual gifts.*

On a scale of 1 to 10 (1 = unknowledgeable; 10 = completely knowledgeable), how much knowledge do you have about spiritual gifts in general?

## For Study and Discussion

Read 1 Corinthians 12:1–11.

1.  Why does Paul not want believers in the church in Corinth to be ignorant about spiritual gifts?
2.  What are spiritual gifts?
3.  Why would it be important for Paul to clarify the truth that there are different gifts, but the same God (vv. 4–6)?
4.  Who gets spiritual gifts? When?
5.  Who decides which people get which gifts?
6.  The root word of the term *spiritual gift* is actually from the word meaning "grace." In what ways is grace involved in the spiritual gifting of believers? What does that mean for those of us who act as though we deserve our gifts?
7.  What is the purpose of the gifts?

Read Romans 12:1–2.

1.  In what way does the concept of surrender apply to our spiritual gifting?
2.  How do Christians renew their minds?

3. Many believers think worship is singing songs to God. How does this passage redefine your idea of worship?

## The Challenge

Surrender your heart and your gifts to God as an act of worship. Ask him to use the next week to reveal what your gift mix is and how he is calling you to use it to influence the lives of others for eternity.

## Before Next Time

Invite a friend, coworker, or neighbor to join your group for the next few sessions of the spiritual adventure.

### Session 3: Making Sense of the Mosaic

## Key Principle

Your spiritual gifts are a treasure. Embarking on the quest to discover your gifts can pull you into the adventure of a lifetime—of an eternity.

## Session Purpose

- To understand the biblical principle of "belonging" to the body of Christ
- To learn how to honor everyone, not just those with gifts considered valuable or popular
- To understand how unity and maturity are achieved through proper use of gifts in the family of God
- To get a feel for your own spiritual gifts and contribution to the community of believers

## Note to Leaders

Read again Landmarks 16 and 17 before this session to familiarize yourself with the list of gifts.

## To Begin

What struck you from the daily readings last week or the beginning of this week? What did you find yourself thinking about or wrestling with? How did God speak to you?

Have you ever quit a team you were a member of? Why did you quit? How did the team feel?

Have you ever started a project without knowing the results? What was that like?

## Diving In

The results of using our gifts in ministry are unity and maturity of the body of Christ. Describe a time in your life when you saw a group of Christians using their gifts to bless others, achieving unity and maturity.

## For Study and Discussion

Look over the list of spiritual gifts (on pages 48–50 and Landmarks 15 and 16).

As you read the list silently, write names of people in your group who you think might exhibit that gift. Try to write each person's name by at least one gift, including your own name. (You may not know everyone very well, so use your best guess based on intuition and discernment.) Focus the group's attention on each member, taking turns speaking the gift or gifts the group thinks each person possesses.

Read 1 Corinthians 12:12–31. If possible, use *The Message* translation of the Bible.

1. Are you ever tempted to think you don't belong to the body because you do not possess an "important" or public gift?
2. Read verse 18 again. Do you believe God knew what he was doing when he gave you the gifts he gave? Why or why not?
3. Has anyone ever communicated that you were not needed because you didn't possess the right gifts? What does that kind of attitude do to the community of believers?
4. There is a portrait of unity in verses 25–26. In what ways can we show greater honor to people with gifts that typically lack honor?

Read Ephesians 4:11–16.
1. Why is the church given the roles of apostles, prophets, evangelists, and pastor-teachers?
2. What is the intended result of believers serving each other?
3. What aspects of maturity are described in verses 14–16? What does maturity look like?

## For Deeper Study
Read 1 Peter 4:1–11.
1. What is the motivation for living for God? Is that a motivation for you?
2. In this passage, why is love so important?
3. How does the use of gifts "administer" God's grace to others?
4. When we practice using our gifts, how seriously should we do it? Why?

## The Challenge

Which gift or gifts has God given to you? Spend time this week praying and talking with others to discover or confirm some of the ways God has gifted you. Ask a few people who are not in your group what gifts they see in you. Record their answers and pray through whether you think they are accurate. Then carve out time this week for extended prayer; try to set aside at least one hour for rest, reflection, and reading. After a time of worship and Bible reading, write on a piece of paper the gifts you think God has given you. Next to each, write the ideas God gives you regarding ways to use your gifts to touch the lives of others.

## Before Next Time

List some ways you might use your gift mix to make a difference in the lives of others. Continue reading the daily devotions. If you miss a few days, skip ahead to the current day and mark those days you missed so you can catch up later.

## Session 4: You Fit in the Family

### Key Principle

Spiritual growth happens in community. Discovering your gifts within a community of faith helps support and safeguard spiritual growth.

### Session Purpose

- To learn the importance of love when living out our Christian faith and using our gifts
- To be challenged to use our gifts appropriately and with love

## Note to Leaders

Follow up with members of your group who have had sporadic attendance. Make sure everyone who misses a session receives a phone call from someone else in the group.

## To Begin

What struck you from the daily readings last week or the beginning of this week? What did you find yourself thinking about or wrestling with? How did God speak to you?

## Testimony

Have someone in your group share a positive experience of using a spiritual gift to meet a human need in Jesus' name. Before the session, ask someone to share for 3 to 4 minutes about a ministry experience that changed the lives of others because he or she chose to use a spiritual gift for God's glory.

## Diving In

- Have you ever said the right thing with the wrong tone of voice and received a cold shoulder or a rebuke? Were you frustrated with yourself? How did you make things right?
- Have you ever felt that a skill you (or someone else) possess was overvalued? Undervalued?
- Have you ever struggled with jealousy of another person's ability?
- Have you ever been rejected because you lacked an ability other people wished you possessed?

## For Study and Discussion

Read 1 Corinthians 13:1–13. We usually think of this passage in terms of marriage and other relationships, but it is written in the context of a discussion on spiritual gifts.

1. How critical is love in using our gifts? What happens when we practice our gifts without love?
2. Think of a spiritual gift you possess. How can you express love through that gift? Is there a way you could be tempted to use that gift without love? How? What are some ways to avoid that pitfall?
3. How is love described? Which aspect of love do you need shown to you right now? Which definition of love do you struggle with the most?
4. One frustrating experience for Christians is waiting—waiting for perfection to come in the midst of imperfection now. This "not yet" struggle of believers is commonplace. Which aspects of waiting for heaven do you struggle with the most?
5. Why did Paul write in verse 13, "the greatest of these is love"? Why is that true?

Read John 13:34–35 and John 15:9–17.
1. What command was Jesus giving to his disciples?
2. What is a key test in understanding whether or not we truly love Jesus?
3. Why is loving each other so important?
4. How will nonbelievers know that we follow Jesus?
5. Is it difficult or easy for you to love other Christians?
6. Which is easier: giving up on the community of Christians and quitting, or loving them?
7. How can we justify quitting if Jesus commands us to love each other?

## The Challenge

Pray this week for those whom you find difficult to love. Ask God to show you ways to love them with his perfect love.

Exercise your gifts in love. When you're tempted to use your gifts in anger or with a bad attitude, check your motives, and ask God to help you love others with the same love you've received from God.

## Before Next Time

Do you tend to err toward hoarding (using your gifts to benefit mostly you) or toward laziness (sitting on the sidelines, not using your gifts)? Avoid both pitfalls and get in the game!

Invite a friend, coworker, or neighbor to church this weekend.

## Session 5: Use What You've Got

Each of us is responsible to develop the gift God has given us. The body of Christ is counting on us! Faithfully develop your gifts; then watch God open doors of opportunity for you, opportunities you never would have imagined.

## Session Purpose

- To understand how to appropriately view ourselves and develop our gifts
- To understand the mandate to use our gifts in ministry to others

## Note to Leaders

After this session, I recommend that your church structure a "ministry fair," where the various opportunities to serve in the church and community can be made available to everyone in the congregation. Remind your group about the upcoming ministry fair. (This is an event our church and many other churches hold a couple times a year during teaching sessions such as this to ensure that people can see the variety of options they have for serving.) Giving your church family an opportunity to see the breadth and depth of ways to serve helps everyone know there is a place for all to serve. We are all needed in the body of Christ!

## To Begin

What struck you from the daily readings last week or the beginning of this week? What did you find yourself thinking about or wrestling with? How did God speak to you?

## Diving In

Have you ever received positive feedback, and you believed it—only to find later that it was not accurate? What happened when you realized that what you did was not as good as you heard initially?

## For Study and Discussion

Read Romans 12:1–8.

1. What pattern of this world should we *not* conform to? Why?

2. Do you tend to think of yourself too highly, not highly enough, or accurately? What does it mean to "think of yourself with sober judgment"?

3. What does it mean that each member of the body belongs to all the others? How would you describe this truth to someone who recently became a Christian?

4. According to verse 6, we have different gifts according to what? Why is this important?

5. In verses 7–8, we are challenged to use the gifts we have. Why would it be significant for Paul to write that

   • those of us with the gift of prophecy should use it in proportion to our faith?

   • those of us with the gift of giving should give generously?

- those of us with leadership gifts ought to use them diligently?
- those of us with the gift of mercy should use it cheerfully?

6. What happens when those gifts are not used as God expects them to be used?

Read Matthew 25:14–30.

1. This striking parable is not necessarily comforting. What point was Jesus making? Why did the master react so strongly when one servant buried what was entrusted to him?

2. Some would argue they don't have time to use their God-given gifts in ministry to others. Scripture leaves no option. Why are the stakes so high when it comes to using our gifts?

## For Deeper Study

Read Matthew 5:14–16. Discuss how these commands affect the area of spiritual gifts and abilities. Have a time of confessional prayer when members of your group confess ways they've buried their gifts and hidden the light of God. Remember God's mercy and our ability as Christians to repent, confess, and move forward in God's grace.

## The Challenge

Share with your group what decisions you've made to diligently use your gifts to minister
- in your workplace or school
- in your local community
- in your church
- in your neighborhood

### Before Next Time

Pray about how you might get involved in changing the lives of others by signing up at your church's office and asking them to help you find a place to serve.

## Session 6: Let God Be the Judge

### Key Principle

God has designed a unique and important place for you in the world. Enter into your calling with confidence and a commitment to use well the treasure he has entrusted to you.

### Session Purpose

- To understand the importance of building your ministry on the foundation of Jesus Christ
- To confirm your current understanding of your calling in life and ministry
- To put into practice one key aspect of the spiritual adventure

### Note to Leaders

This is your last formal session during the spiritual adventure. Look over Session 6 and plan as a group your celebration event at the end of this session.

### To Begin

What struck you from the daily readings last week or the beginning of this week? What did you find yourself thinking about or wrestling with? How did God speak to you?

## Testimony

Have someone from your group share a brief testimony about how the spiritual adventure has touched his or her life. Before the session, ask that person to share for 3 to 4 minutes the ways God has touched his or her life in this place and time through the teaching and reading, and through believers.

## Diving In

Have you ever run out of gasoline before you arrived at your destination? What happened? How did you get help? How can you prevent stopping before you reach the spiritual destinations God has for you right now?

This spiritual adventure lasts for six weeks—a relatively small snapshot in time when compared to your entire life. What do you wish you had more time to focus on? Are you able to do that later, after the adventure? What will you do to extend the benefits of this adventure after it is finished?

## For Study and Discussion

Read 1 Corinthians 3:10–4:5.

1. In serving God by ministering to other people, what would it look like to build a foundation on something other than the rock of Jesus Christ?
2. In 3:13, what does this mean: "It will be revealed with fire"?
3. Have you ever ministered to others from a bad foundation or with bad motives? What happened? How did you feel afterward?
4. Do you sense you're building your ministry on Jesus' foundation or on a foundation of wood, hay, or straw?
5. The apostle Paul's character had come under attack at the church in Corinth. In this section, Paul was clearly

defending his position as an apostle. In 4:3, why did Paul say, "I care very little if I am judged by you"?

6. How important are others' perceptions of your ministry? When is their input important? When is it not important?

7. When in the past have you experienced someone ministering to others with impure motives? What happened? How did you process and move past that experience?

8. When you suspect that someone is ministering to others out of motives that are less than pure, would the truth of 4:5 be helpful to you? Why or why not?

Read Colossians 1:9–14.

1. As a group, list the four key principles involved in living a life worthy of the Lord and pleasing to him.

2. Which of the four is easiest for you? Which is most difficult? Which would you most like to see increase in your life?

3. How important do you think it is to minister out of an overflow in your life? Do you think you can sustain ministry long-term without vital spiritual life in the four key areas outlined by Paul in Colossians 1? Why or why not?

Read 2 Timothy 1:3–14.

1. What do you need to do to fan your gifts into flame?

2. Do you ever struggle with timidity when it comes to using your gifts? How can you more fully experience power, love, and self-discipline as you serve God, using your gifts and abilities?

3. In the process of serving God, what do we entrust to him? What does he entrust to us?

## For Deeper Study

Read 1 Corinthians 9:24–10:13.

1. The idea of competition is often not readily valued in Christian circles. Why do you think Paul commanded us to run in such a way as to win? What did he mean? What did he not mean?

2. When you think about your ministry to others, would you describe your preparation as strict training? Why or why not? Do you consider preparation critical to the ministry dynamic, or does God simply bless us with the words to say at any given moment through his Spirit?

3. What would it mean to be disqualified? Is it possible to conduct yourself in a way that disqualifies you from serving God in any visible capacity? Would you then never be accountable to use your gifts in ministry again? Explore this concept of disqualification as a group.

4. At the beginning of chapter 10, Paul gave an example from the Old Testament about people of God who were disqualified. He then spoke of their example and how we could learn from them. What key principles did Paul highlight?

5. What should we do when we face strong temptation? What should we look for?

## The Challenge

Think back on the entire spiritual adventure. What is the most important thing you've learned or been reminded of? What one thing does God want you to carry forward as you serve him?

## Additional Idea

Plan a celebration event together. Choose from one of the following ideas or make up your own:

- Come together for a family-style potluck at someone's home.
- Reserve a back room at a local restaurant and have dinner together.
- Go see a movie together, and go out for ice cream afterward.
- Take a day trip together to a favorite nearby destination.
- Go away for a weekend together (camping, hiking, staying at a retreat house or motel) to fish, hike, ski, or do whatever else would be fun at that time of year.

When you gather for the celebration, try to incorporate the following agenda:

- Offer thanks for what God has taught you. Ask each other, "What are you thankful for as a result of this spiritual adventure?"
- Ask each other, "How are you *thinking* more clearly, *feeling* more deeply, or *acting* more consistently because of this spiritual adventure?"
- Ask each other, "What gifts were discovered and affirmed in community that you had not considered before the adventure began?"
- Have each member create a journal entry about the adventure with thoughts, prayers, thanks, and photographs. Make a collage for your group and frame it to mark the moment together.
- Consider continuing your group, class, or team. Plan the next curriculum and topic, and schedule the day and time to begin meeting.

# APPENDIX

There are a number of online spiritual gifts assessment tools. The following are several sites where you can take a spiritual gifts test to begin discovering your spiritual gifts:

- Ministry Tools Resource Center—Online Spiritual Gifts Test Inventory
  http://mintools.com/spiritual-gifts-test.htm

- Eleven Talents Ministry—Spiritual Gifts Test
  http://www.eleventalents.com/giftstest.htm

- Team Ministry—Spiritual Gifts Analysis
  http://www.churchgrowth.org/cgi-cg/gifts.cgi?intro=1

- Lay Ministry—Downloadable Spiritual Gifts Test and Workbook
  http://www.layministry.com/

# REFERENCES

Collins, Jim. *Good to Great: Why Some Companies Make the Leap . . . and Others Don't* (New York: Harper Collins, 2001).

Jackson, John. *Pastorpreneur: Outreach Beyond Business as Usual* (Minden, NV: VisionQuest Ministries, 2003).

Jackson, John and Lorraine Bossé-Smith. *Leveraging Your Leadership Style: Maximize Your Influence by Discovering the Leader Within* (Nashville: Abingdon Press, 2008).

Omartian, Stormie. *The Power of a Praying Wife* (Eugene, OR: Harvest House Publishers, 1997).

Sutherland, Dave and Kirk Nowery, *The 33 Laws of Stewardship: Principles for a Life of True Fulfillment* (Camarillo, CA: Spire Resources, 2003).

Warren, Rick. *Purpose Driven Church: Growth Without Compromising Your Message and Mission* (Grand Rapids, MI: Zondervan, 1995).

# Also Available

This how-to for church growth outlines principles of growth for all sizes of congregations, while emphasizing that church growth is not about numbers, but about fulfilling God's vision for your church's impact on the world.

**Paperback, 176 pages, 5.5 x 8.5**
**ISBN: 978-1-60657-107-1**
**Retail: $15.99**

**Available for purchase at book retailers everywhere.**

This book explores thirty-one practical ways the resurrection changed the lives of early believers and can transform us today. *This Changes Everything* provides the foundation and understanding to help and equip you to live the power of the resurrection.

**Paperback, 176 pages,**
**5.125 x 7.625**
**ISBN: 978-1-60657-085-2**
**Retail: $10.99**

**Available for purchase at book retailers everywhere.**